HERBS

HERBS

EXCITING RECIPES FOR COOKING WITH HERBS

LINDA TUBBY PHOTOGRAPHY BY PETER CASSIDY

RYLAND
PETERS
& SMALL

LONDON NEW YORK

First published in Great Britain in 2004
by Ryland Peters & Small
Kirkman House, 12–14 Whitfield Street
London W1T 2RP
www.rylandpeters.com

10 9 8 7 6 5 4 3 2 1

Text © Linda Tubby 2004
Design and photographs
© Ryland Peters & Small 2004

ISBN 1 84172 567 6

A catalogue record for this book is available from the British Library

Printed and bound in China

Senior Designer Steve Painter
Commissioning Editor Elsa Petersen-Schepelern
Production Patricia Harrington
Art Director Gabriella Le Grazie
Publishing Director Alison Starling

Food Stylist Linda Tubby
Stylist Róisín Nield
Indexer Diana LeCore

AN
641·65-7

Dedication

For my sons Dan and Ben, with love.

Acknowledgements

My thanks go first to photographer Peter Cassidy, whose lovely and sensitive work has made this book so special. To Kate, his assistant, without whom we would all be lost – bless you. Special thanks to Elsa for being a most encouraging and supportive editor and so knowledgeable about all sorts of odd things. To Steve Painter, for all his creative thoughts, enthusiasm and superb book designing (he also knows a thing or two about gardening, which was handy). To Róisín Nield, for beautiful prop styling and always knowing just what to bring.

Dan at Mortimer and Bennet for his food advice. Phil, Gary and Eddie at Covent Garden Fisheries for always ensuring I had pretty happy fish. Phalida Chard for all things Thai. Paul Gayler for being such a good influence, to many more people who gave advice, and to Lesley Faddy for rocket fuel and more.

My family for putting up with herb pots and for doing without joined-up meals. My Mam, my friends, and supporters who are forever there and great. Jerry for techy support. Finally, thanks to those wonderful herbs for always being right outside my door. Everyone at Ryland Peters & Small, who have been so helpful, especially Sharon Ashman for her help with editing and Gabriella le Grazie for her basil enthusiasm.

Notes

• All spoon measurements are level unless otherwise stated.

• Ingredients in this book are available from larger supermarkets, specialist greengrocers, garden centres and nurseries. Some of the more unusual herbs must be sought out in Asian markets, or grown in your own garden. See page 142 for mail order sources.

• Fresh herbs are preferred for the recipes in this book, and most are available year round. If using dried herbs for any reason, use about one-third of the measure mentioned. Some herbs, such as thyme, tarragon, oregano and bay leaves have specific uses in their dried forms, so buy them from a source with a fast turnover. Like spices, they lose pungency with age, so buy little and often.

• Ovens should be preheated to the specified temperature. Recipes in this book were tested using a conventional oven. If using a fan oven, cooking times should be changed according to the manufacturer's instructions.

• For all recipes requiring dough or batter, liquid measurements are given as a guide. Always add liquid gradually to achieve the desired consistency, rather than adding it all at once. Use your eyes and your sense of touch to achieve the best results. If you don't use the type of flour specified in a recipe, the result may be affected.

CONTENTS

INTRODUCTION

Fresh herbs have such a natural appeal in the kitchen adding a vast range of exciting flavour dimensions to the dishes we cook. With so many exotic fresh herbs now available from all over the world and all the hundreds of different varieties we can grow at home, cooking with herbs has never been so inspiring. They thrill with their visual beauty and a variety of sensational aromas – from rounded cushions of wild oregano on hot Greek hillsides to the creamy-white, frothy feminine flower heads of sweet cicely growing by streams and along country roadsides in springtime. Once seen, who can forget fields of French lavender growing in swathes across the landscape or Italian basil with shiny, brilliant-green leaves growing in abundance just waiting to enliven a dish of ripe tomatoes? I love the markets of South-east Asia, which groan with huge bunches of flowering chives, lemongrass and Thai basil, so firm and fresh, just begging to give their heady aroma to flavour a tangy stir-fry or curry.

Herbs have been around as a natural resource for many thousands of years. Many of them started out life in the sunny climate of the Mediterranean and were carried to other parts of the world by invaders and explorers, who spread the seeds of many of the familiar herbs we use today.

Fresh herbs are preferred for the recipes in this book, and most are available year round. However, this wasn't always so, and various forms of drying have been evolved, all of which try to preserve the flavour, aroma, and (formerly) the medicinal qualities of the herbs in question. Some, especially woody herbs, respond well to drying. Other, softer ones, such as basil, don't. A modern invention, freeze-drying, has improved their prospects somewhat, but I think that, if possible, use herbs fresh. This is not to ignore the fact that some, such as thyme, tarragon, oregano, and bay leaves, do have specific uses in their dried forms, so if you plan to cook recipes using this form of herb, buy from a source with a fast turnover. Like spices, dried herbs lose pungency with age, so buy little and often.

All these wonderful fresh herbs we now have at our green fingertips bring a special flavour to our cookery endeavours as well as an extra hidden dimension – they help our bodies deal with the food we eat and bring added vitamins and minerals to our diet. In days gone by, people gradually acquired an understanding of herbs both for their culinary and medicinal uses, a wisdom passed on from generation to generation. Sage was known to aid digestion so it was added to rich foods; thyme, because of its powerful antiseptic qualities, was used to marinate meat to stop it spoiling long before refrigeration; and dill was used to ease the pain of teething infants and to aid digestion.

The Romans especially used herbs not only in their food but also to nurture mind, body and spirit. Their huge armies made great use of them, for at that time herbs were the only medicine available. It's exciting that herbs are as adaptable as ever they were, playing their dual role for us today as our food and medicine.

KNOW YOUR HERBS

bay leaves

hyssop

lavender

rosemary

savory

thyme

STRONG WOODY HERBS

Bay leaves come from the same family as avocado and cinnamon. The bay tree was originally a wild plant of the Mediterranean, where it thrives more pungently and powerfully than anywhere else. Greek and Roman heroes were crowned with wreaths of bay leaves as a symbol of excellence.

When you crush the leaves, the aromas range from grassy and floral to bitter – as a flavouring herb, they stand up to long cooking, which brings out their sweet mellowness.

Infuse a leaf or two in milk and cream for savoury or sweet dishes or use a sprig in a bowl of red wine marinade with garlic and onions. When cooking cabbage, cauliflower or other strong-smelling vegetables, add a bay leaf to diminish the odour.

Rosemary has been a culinary and medicinal herb since ancient Greek and Roman times. The Romans thought so highly of it they dedicated it to Venus, the Goddess of Love. It is also thought to improve the memory – as Ophelia said so sadly in Shakespeare's *Hamlet*, 'rosemary is for remembrance'.

Apart from the classic partnerships with roast lamb or monkfish, the leaves are also capable of delivering some delicious flavours to puddings. Put the flowers or leaves in a pot of sugar for two weeks and use to make meringue or syrups, or warm the leaves and flowers with honey to pour over grilled figs, melon or orange salad.

Sage – from the Latin word *salvere* meaning 'to save' – was and still is a highly valued medicinal herb, as well as a prime candidate for the award for one of the best culinary herbs.

It is known as the 'herb of the heart' and – even more astonishing – chewing the leaves is said to make teeth white and shiny.

Sage is a popular herb in many regions of Italy. Its pungent robustness adds a new dimension to buttery dishes and many others, including my own favourite – rare char-grilled calves' liver with sage leaves fried in melted butter with a little dusting of hot paprika on the plate. In Tuscany, butter is infused with sage to serve with ravioli and gnocchi.

In Germany, it is cooked with eel, helping the digestive system cope with the richness of the dish. It makes a delicious flavouring for apple jelly to serve with pork, rich potato dishes with cream are transformed, while the flowers can be used to flavour bread dough, or to decorate the top of the loaf.

Sage, like many woody herbs, can stand up to long, slow cooking without losing its strength. In spring, sage has a gentle, mild aroma, but by the summer, when the flowers are just in bud, its volatile oils have matured in the heat of the sun. This is the combination that can create the 'medicine cabinet' effect that is too overpowering for food, unless used with a delicate hand.

To care for sage, put bunches of leaves in a jug of shallow water with just the very ends

of the stalks in the water, put a plastic bag over the top and when the leaves have perked up take the bag off and leave the jug of herbs on the kitchen table as an edible decoration. I like to keep them this way rather than in the refrigerator, where the leaves turn limp and sad.

Purple sage can be used as common sage, but it is not as pungent, so it is good pan-fried, or dipped in batter and deep-fried.

Pineapple sage has red-edged, pointed, oval leaves with red stems and scarlet flowers in winter. Early in the season the leaves have a strong pineapple flavour when crushed. This flavour diminishes after flowering. Use the leaves instead of tansy in the Panna Cotta recipe on page 123. There are many scented sages you can plant in your garden, and they are worth some experimentation as culinary ammunition.

Savory or *sarriete* – its charming French name – was introduced into northern Europe by the Romans, who used this highly aromatic herb as a peppery, spicy flavouring. It was commonly used to ease digestion after the enjoyment of certain challenging foods and, as if that weren't enough, it was also considered an aphrodisiac.

Summer savory is an annual and is known as the bean herb because it eases flatulence. The flavour of the tender leaves is similar to thyme. I like to use the leaves and flowers – white or pale pink – with beans, lentils, char-grilled fish and vegetables.

Winter savory is evergreen, with lilac or white flowers, and a little stronger and a bit more resinous than summer savory with a flavour similar to thyme. It suits bean dishes as well as char-grilled meat and fish. A commercially grown savory is now available in supermarkets but it hasn't the same strength as homegrown.

Thyme from the Greek *thymos* – 'to perfume' – has so many varieties, full of character and all with their own subtle aroma and flavour.

The ancient Egyptians and Greeks knew the powerful antiseptic and preservative qualities of thyme and its ability to stimulate the brain and improve the memory. Roman cooks used it to preserve their meat: those strong antiseptic qualities delayed spoiling.

In the 17th century, cooking with thyme was believed to make fairies visible – I like that.

Lemon thyme tastes strongly of citrus and is delicious grilled with peaches and figs or stuffed inside a fish. Add a few sprigs to a marinade for lamb along with oil and black pepper – let chill in the refrigerator for 24 hours, adding salt for the last 30 minutes as you let the lamb return to room temperature before cooking.

Hyssop, a common Mediterranean shrub, was a sacred herb in ancient Greece. It is a good foil for rich pork dishes and oily fish, because it aids digestion. The leaves have a minty, anise-like flavour with a little sage note, while the white, pink or purple flowers have a minty taste. The leaves are still quite potent in winter and add a warm spiciness to poached fruits.

When chopped and used as a rub, its strength is the perfect partner for game dishes. But take care – like all the woody herbs, its strength varies depending on the season, and a heavy hand can ruin a dish.

Lavender was highly prized by the Greeks and Romans, who liked the scent and healing qualities in their bath water – its name is derived from the Latin *lavare* meaning 'to wash'. Though lavender has always been considered terribly English, my memories of France are of lavender, with drifts of it colouring the view to infinity.

The culinary talents of lavender have been known for centuries and it's becoming a top herb again. Use the flowers to flavour sugar and to make biscuits, syrups, ice creams and in a more savoury context for stuffings and sauces. Well-known British chef Paul Gayler of London's Lanesborough hotel grinds down the buds and calls it 'pollen', which he mixes with butter and puts under the skin of a chicken to roast – quite delicious. I grind the flowers with salt and use as a rub for meat. Use the leaves to flavour game and roast with a leg of lamb as you would rosemary. It's very potent, so use it sparingly.

I have a soft spot for the fresh blossoms, which I snatch from under the bees' noses and scatter over summer strawberries along with a dusting of scented sugar (the berries can take the overkill) and a dollop of whipped cream.

Lavender was used in love spells to attract men. So if you feel the need, get out your cooking pots and start weaving the magic.

SOFT LEAFY HERBS

Basil takes its name from the Greek *basileus*, meaning 'king'. It is native to India, where it is sacred and known as *tulsi*. It was first brought to Egypt around 3000 years ago, then on to Rome and so to all parts of southern Europe. These days it grows wherever the climate suits.

Many cooks have a rule that basil must only be torn, not cut. Metal reacts with the plant juices, turning the cut edges black and bitter. If the leaf is torn, the tear takes the natural line of the cell structure.

Greek or bush basil is very bushy with tiny pointed leaves and white flowers. It is grown throughout Greece in gardens or pots near doorways as a sign of welcome and in churches it can be found just below the altar in its spiritual role as holy basil.

The common basil we know as **sweet or Italian basil** is not shy about throwing its peppery, minty clove-like scent around when warmed by the sun, but when cold in the confines of the larder it can smell of cats.

Lettuce basil is a large-leaved variety. Use whole leaves in wrappings or as stuffings, or tear them into salads.

Purple basil or **opal basil** has pinkish-purple, and in some cases almost black, leaves. If it flops, plunge into hand-hot water for 15 minutes – not only does this bring it back to life, it intensifies its colour quite dramatically.

Basil is said to create understanding between people. It also has a raunchy reputation in Spain where ladies of ill repute use it to entice clients.

Asia has its own family of basils, and these are listed on page 16.

Borage was taken all over Europe by the Roman legions. Roman soldiers believed it gave them great courage – something obviously worked, as they rampaged their way across the known world for over 500 years.

Young, fresh borage has strong cucumber-flavoured leaves – delicious dipped in light batter and deep-fried. Float the star-like purple flowers in drinks or freeze them in ice cubes to chill summer drinks – a classic when served with that English favourite, Pimm's.

Chervil was introduced as a flavouring herb to Western Europe by the invading Roman legions. They carried it from the Caucasus and the Middle East to western Europe where it settled into common use, especially in France and Belgium. It is part of the herb quartet that flavours the classic French dish *omelette au fines herbes* – to which its contribution is important, because a little chervil accentuates the flavour of the other three herbs. It makes a delicate soup and when added to young carrots, it reaches dizzy heights.

Always add chervil to a hot dish at the very last moment because its flavour is destroyed by prolonged cooking. Use the tangles of lacy leaves in salads to maximize invaluable nutritional benefits.

Chervil has a sweet, mildly anise flavour with a twang of fruity wine. Though it looks delicate, it's a brave little herb and when grown in the garden is a good deal hardier than any commercially grown specimen. It was available in supermarkets for a while, but the poor little thing wasn't quite strong enough for the tough packaged life. You can find it in good greengrocers who know how to deal with its delicate demeanour.

basil

chervil

coriander

dill

fennel

lovage

Coriander is the herb mentioned in the Bible and in Sanskrit texts and was found in Egyptian tombs in seed form. Its popularity has stood the test of time, considering it has also had the worst press in the world. We love it and hate it with equal passion. I'm firmly in the former camp, but feel I always have to ask if everyone likes it before mixing handfuls into a dish. Although coriander must not be cooked to death, it really needs that brief assignation with the warmth of the food to bring out its fullness. On the other hand, its idiosyncratic flavour in fresh salsa is not to be missed.

Coriander was brought to Europe by late bronze-age nomads to flavour their barley gruel, while the Spaniards carried it to Mexico and Peru, where it became an indispensable partner to their much loved chilli. In Britain, it was commercially grown in the 19th century for the seed, which was used as a supporting flavour for gin.

Dill started out in the Middle East in biblical times. It migrated with travellers into Europe, North and South America, further east into Asia as well as north to Scandinavia.

Its name comes appropriately from the old Norse word *dylla* meaning 'to lull'. The leaves have a sweet, almost alcoholic flavour, with vague hints of anise that aren't as strong as fennel, but similar to caraway in taste.

It is used in Scandinavia with salmon, carrots and beetroot or tossed into new potatoes with butter. Polish cooks use it with sour cream, hard-boiled eggs and gherkins. The Greeks like to partner it with broad beans and in Iran it's

eaten raw, along with other herbs on the table throughout the meal. Dill is used as a vegetable in South-east Asia, where it's always cooked and goes by the name *paksi* or *pak chi lao*.

Graceful **fennel**, with its feathery foliage under an umbrella of yellow flowers, was used by the Greeks to suppress the appetite.

Fennel will keep in a plastic bag in the salad drawer of the refrigerator for four days providing it's not wet, when it becomes slimy very quickly.

Fennel is the perfect herb stuffed inside or sprinkled on top of oily fish, and the clean fresh flavour is delicious tossed through char-grilled vegetables.

Lovage, sometimes known as sea parsley (it grows wild on sea cliffs and coastlines), has a strong celery scent, and is known for its 'meaty' protein flavour. When young, the leaves taste salty and lemony and are good in salads or with vegetable and bean casseroles. When the plant grows tall and the leaves become slightly bitter, use them just for stews.

It is good with potato soup and I love it cooked in the oven with lentils and onions.

Like many herbs, lovage was grown in the earliest monastic physic gardens for medicinal purposes. It was thought to be good for digestive problems and to relieve stomach cramps. At one time it was thought to be an aphrodisiac – hence the name.

Mint was introduced to Europe by the Romans and has remained the most popular herb in the world. Peppermint tea of course is the drink of

choice throughout the Middle East as it is as stimulating as coffee. It was said to restore and revive the spirit and excite the appetite.

Infuse the leaves in boiling water for five minutes to overcome nausea. Add to green tea as in Morocco, or use in iced mint tea, made by adding a handful of bruised mint leaves to a pot of Chinese green tea with the juice of a lime and some honey. Chill well, adding ice cubes, if you like. Another great summer drink is mint julep – mash mint leaves with sugar and mix with crushed ice and bourbon.

Spearmint or garden mint is used in classic mint sauce with roast lamb. The perfect mint sauce is made by pouring boiling water over a handful of chopped mint with sugar. Let cool, then add cider vinegar to taste and serve with a silver or non-reactive spoon. Mint is also a favourite in kebabs, the comfort food of the Middle East, the raita of India and the *sauce paloise* of France.

Apple mint has a soft grey-green fleshy leaf with a wonderful apple mint aroma and flavour. Use whole sprigs when cooking peas, potatoes and beans.

Sweet marjoram, now found all over the Mediterranean and western Asia, was introduced to Europe in the Middle Ages from North Africa. Use in dishes that don't need lengthy cooking, such as soufflés and light food. The leaves become floppy quickly, so add to salads at the last minute. Marjoram's generic name is 'oregano', while confusingly oregano's other name is 'wild marjoram'. Sweet marjoram looks delicate with light-green, soft leaves and a

marjoram

oregano

mint

young flat leaf parsley

sweet cicely

tarragon

beige–pink stalk. The leaves are sweetly scented, with white or pinky-purple flowers. It has a more fleshy and tender look to it than the stronger looking relative, pot marjoram, also known as French marjoram.

The antiseptic qualities for which this genus was famous meant that it was used as a strewing herb, scattered around kitchens to keep them sweet-smelling. As a result, it was a prominent crop in the kitchen gardens from Renaissance times.

I have grown pot marjoram for many years and it looks very similar to oregano, except the leaves are a lighter green and the flowers tend to be paler. It has a slightly tougher leaf than sweet marjoram, and so it can be used more robustly in tomato sauces and dishes that are cooked a little longer. I use it in a meatball mixture together with mint and pine nuts.

Golden marjoram has a very soft, pale, greeny-gold leaf with white flowers. It grows so well for me in big fat cushions and is so lush that it's difficult for me to cut into it. But this I must do as the flavour is excellent and stands up well to cooking when added ten minutes before the end.

Oregano, or wild marjoram, as it is sometimes known, is a woody perennial, and the hotter the sun the stronger the flavour. This genus belongs to the mint family. Italians use the flower heads just before they bloom as well as the leaves to flavour dishes.

The many wild species of oregano are known collectively as 'rigani', which grows wild on hillsides and mountains throughout Greece. It's the wild species (not grown commercially) which is harvested when in bud and dried for maximum aroma. We love to bring it back from holidays in Greece by the suitcase-full.

In Latin America and the Mediterranean, oregano is used as we use parsley. It is an essential ingredient in Italian cooking and a favourite herb in Greek cuisine – where would they be without it for tomato sauces and salads?

Parsley was a native of the eastern Mediterranean and was brought to western Europe in the 16th century where it began to grow so naturally and happily in rough places that it became known as 'rock celery'. The Greeks considered parsley to have too many associations with the devil, so preferred to keep its use to the medicine cabinet. The Romans, however, were happy to cook with it – how clued up they were – it's now considered the most indispensable culinary herb.

Flat leaf parsley (or French, Italian or Continental parsley, as it's often called) is essential to many traditional flavouring mixtures. My favourite is Italian gremolata – a mix of parsley, chopped garlic and lemon zest, which is sprinkled over finished dishes. The French version is *persillade*, traditionally made without lemon.

One of my favourite uses of parsley is in *beurre de gascogne* – lots of blanched garlic and freshly chopped parsley mixed with duck or goose fat and mixed into a simple cassoulet at the last moment. I make *salmoriglio* – a mixture of salt, garlic, lemon juice, olive oil and parsley, which is fabulous for sardines and fresh anchovies. Parsley (and mint) is also the essential herb in tabbouleh where classically the herbs are the dish and the grains of bulghur wheat are included simply to stop the juices from the other ingredients falling to the bottom of the bowl.

Curly leaf parsley isn't the most fashionable herb and many discount it, but the flavour, when well grown, is iron-laden and sweet. I love it deep-fried to a crispness, so it crumbles in the mouth like Cantonese crispy seaweed. It also holds up well to cooking in stuffing, but must be finely chopped, or the texture can be prickly. If you grow it at home, make sure the leaves are picked when tender. Like other parsley varieties, it contains masses of chlorophyll, the bright-green leaf juice which is packed with goodness.

Sweet cicely, sometimes known as liquorice root, is a native of northern Europe. This is a herb you must grow yourself, because as yet no one sells it by the bunch. This is a shame – its qualities demand that it should be in more prominent use. Its firm, chervil-like leaves and froth of white flowers have a sweet anise and liquorice flavour, so it tastes very good in all things sweet. It loves the companionship of sharp fruits in dishes like crumbles, reducing the acidity, so you need less sugar.

Add the leaves to vegetable soups right at the end of cooking to sweeten and bring out their flavour. I like the leaves in green salads and with grilled goats' cheese. The leaves and flowers also make fantastic tempura with extra leaves infused in a syrup, then strained to use as a dip.

Tansy is a native of Europe and the Greeks and Romans considered a symbol of immortality. To my mind it's like coriander in that it is either loved or loathed. It is very deep in flavour, quite unforgettable. Tansy was the name of the herb as well as the name of the pudding it flavoured – eaten at Easter time, often in the form of bread-like cakes. At other times it appeared in rich mousse-like creamy puddings. Rubbed on lamb it gives a similar flavour to rosemary. In the 17th century it was stir-fried with oranges and sugar.

Tansy has strong antiseptic qualities and before there was such a thing as refrigeration, it was used to wrap meat to repel flies. I use only the very young leaves for flavouring the pudding on page 123. Like many bitter herbs, it has a reputation as a digestive stimulant – people with a sensitive constitution may like to substitute bay or thyme instead.

Tarragon is the aristocrat of the herb garden. The aromatic, shiny, smooth, light-green leaves are the only soft leaf herb that can withstand long cooking. In fact, I think cooking it mellows and warms the flavour, losing the harsher side of its character. This herb makes famous pairings with chicken or rich cream sauces. The pungent, bossy, anise flavour turns saintly and mellow after 30 minutes in the oven with chicken pieces, white wine and double cream. Remove the branch of tarragon towards the end of cooking and add a second hit of it about five minutes before the end of the cooking time.

The flavour of tarragon is at its most pungent in high summer. It can have a numbing effect on the tongue when chewed raw, and is quite alcoholic in flavour – like pastis, but without the water to temper its strength.

Many gardeners have been disappointed when they discover they have the tasteless Russian variety, rather than the glorious French. Take care when you buy small plants – scratch and sniff the leaves to make sure.

Tarragon is one of those herbs that survives the drying process. French roast chicken with dried tarragon is delicious – the version in which many people first taste this wonderful herb.

THE ONION FAMILY

Garlic is the ultimate herb grown for flavouring and as a vegetable in its own right. The active substance in garlic is ailicun, which comes to the fore when the cloves are chopped or crushed, this is the medicinally active part and creates the garlic odour. Garlic is at its most beneficial to health when eaten raw, but still retains many benefits when cooked. Russians eat it to keep old age at bay.

If you grow your own, divide the cloves from the bulb and plant them in autumn for the next year. They produce a delicious crop, and also keep insects away from other plants. Young green garlic is useful in many dishes for its mild flavour and also makes a delicious soup. Extreme temperature change can cause garlic to take on a hotter taste. The variety grown in Thailand has a less pungent flavour than its Western relative. Leave some plants to flower – they are beautiful with large pompoms, like big chive flowers.

Chives were brought back to Europe from the East by Marco Polo in the 13th century and have since become indispensable in the kitchen, in the same way as garlic and onions. Some people say they shouldn't be cooked, but I find they are a perfect flavouring for soufflés and savoury tarts with fillings based on eggs, cream or cheese. Where would we be without chives sprinkled over new potatoes or snipped over hot baked potato with sour cream?

If you're a gardener, there are many varieties available, some with white flowers, but the common chive with its lilac-pink pompom flower heads is hard to beat. I use these flowers all through the spring to scatter over salads and grilled dishes or any dish where a hint of onion flavour works.

After cutting the leaves from the plant, wrap them in damp kitchen paper, then put them in a plastic bag and store in the salad drawer of the refrigerator.

Chinese chives, also known as garlic chives, have been cultivated for centuries in China, Japan and Vietnam. One variety has flat leaves and is sold either with just leaves, or with the large buds or flowers. They give a mild garlic flavour and can be used like common chives or in stir-fries and rice dishes. These can be bought from Asian stores bound in long bundles.

Also in Chinese markets, you will find a variety that is blanched under cloches to whiten them, and these are considered a delicacy.

Flowering chives or **kuchai** are grown specifically for their flowering stems, in bud or flower form. The stems and flowers are chopped into stir-fry dishes. These have an ultra-powerful, pungently garlic smell, a bit like wild garlic, but cooking tempers the smell and flavour.

Wild garlic or **ramsons**, with its spear-like leaves, is found growing wild in muddy, shady places. Take care when gathering them, and wash thoroughly before use. They are also cultivated and, in season, are sometimes sold in gourmet stores. Both flowers and leaves are edible, but the leaves are best eaten before the plant flowers.

The leaves are lovely as a wrapping for steamed fish. The stunning starry flowers have a pungent flavour and are good used in a salad of bitter leaves tossed with goats' cheese and nuts.

Chop and wilt the leaves with baby spinach to fold through stuffed pasta just before serving.

CITRUS FLAVOURED HERBS

Lemon verbena, a native of Chile and Argentina, was brought to Europe in the 18th century by the Spaniards. It has strong, lance-shaped leaves with an intensely fresh lemon aroma, at its best when the flowers are on the verge of blooming. However, even in winter, the few remaining dried-out leaves left on a plant still retain a strong fragrance when crushed.

Use lemon verbena in fish dishes and with duck. I infuse the leaves in cream to make panna cotta (page 123) and use it to poach peaches in summer, then infuse it in sugar and chilled wine to make a syllabub for the topping. A few of the delicate pink flowers sprinkled over the top reinforces the flavour.

To help insomnia, make a tisane (herb tea) from crushed fresh leaves, and sip the strained liquid last thing at night.

Lemon balm is also known as balm, lime balm, bee balm or melissa (the Greek word for honey bee). The plants were used by bee keepers in the 17th and 18th centuries to keep their bees well behaved and close to the hives.

The serrated, slightly hairy leaves look very much like small nettle leaves and in summer the plant is covered with tiny white flowers. The aroma can be quite overpowering in old, tough plants, especially those grown in pots.

Lemon balm is wonderful to flavour jellies, vinegar, vegetables, fresh fruits and cold drinks.

In the 13th century, lemon balm was mixed with honey and used to make a tisane. It was said to chase away dark thoughts, strengthen a stressed nervous system and, above all, to keep you young. Today, herbalists still use it to calm and soothe.

Vietnamese balm, is grown and used in the West. Although not from the same family as lemon balm, it has similar attributes and could be used as a substitute.

Remember also **lemon geranium** (below), **kaffir lime leaves** and **lemongrass** (page 16). Other herbs have varieties with citrus flavours, such as **lemon thyme** (page 10).

FLOWER AND FRUIT SCENTED HERBS

Scented geranium leaves have an intense scent associated with the variety. **Rose** smells of roses, **lemon** of lemon, and there are **apple, mint** or **nutmeg** scented geraniums. The flowers, unlike other herbs, have no scent at all but are edible and can be used to decorate puddings or salads. Use the fresh leaves to scent sugar stored in a jar – the results can be used for custards, syrups, meringues, ice creams and jellies. The leaves are pretty pressed into the top of a cake and covered with a dusting of caster sugar before baking.

The botanical name of the **pot marigold** is Calendula from the Latin *calendae* meaning 'little clock', so called because it flowers all year round in its natural habitat in the Mediterranean. It opens at sunrise and closes at sunset. This is one of my favourite herbs and my best medicinal support for cuts – calendula tincture travels with me whenever my cook's knives come too. It also has an almost magical ability to keep blackfly from my garden. I love its simple, bright, cheery flowers in orange and yellow – so good to look at in the garden and for flavour and colour in food. Fresh and dried petals have been added to the cooking pot since the Middle Ages hence the name

'pot marigold'. The flowers have a warm, peppery, salty taste and work wonders with feta cheese and pine nuts. Teamed with ricotta in a stuffing for courgette flowers, they are sublime, and good in herb omelettes, too. The colour produced from the petals is the poor man's saffron, giving a wonderful orange tone with a subtle flavour, though not quite as spicily pungent as saffron.

Nasturtium is a relative of watercress and is also known as Indian cress. It is a native of South America, introduced into Spain from Peru in the 16th century and reaching other European countries 100 years later. Flowers and leaves have an intense, pungent, mustardy, peppery flavour. The flamboyant yellow, orange and red of the flowers make them the ideal spicy snap for many recipes, especially salads – and they look beautiful, too.

Viola, also known as wild pansy, heartsease or Johnny jump-up, is a native of Europe. The common name 'pansy' is from the French word *pensée,* meaning a thought or remembrance of love. Although you shouldn't eat too many at once, they are good in salads, in stuffing or crystallized and used to decorate puddings.

An infusion made from viola flowers was said to mend a broken heart.

Sweet violets are the purple violets classically used to flavour violet cream chocolates.

shiso leaf

epazote

curry leaf

kaffir lime leaf

lemongrass

vietnamese coriander (laksa leaf)

EXOTIC NEW ARRIVALS

More and more unusual herbs appear in our restaurants and cookbooks as chefs and food writers travel the world, and immigrants open eateries in their new countries. Whenever you see these ingredients for sale, ask the shopkeeper how they are used and how to cook with them. They will always be helpful, and all good cooks are imbued with the spirit of adventure.

Lemongrass can be grown in a greenhouse, or outdoors if you live in a mild climate. It's also widely available in Asian markets. Use the bottom 5 cm or so of the bulb, and peel off the outer couple of leaves. Either bruise the whole grass and remove it before serving, or cut it very finely, then mash even more finely with a mortar and pestle. Lemongrass stalks can also be used as kebab sticks. Freeze what you don't use – it can be used straight from frozen.

Kaffir lime leaves are the beautiful dark, glossy green leaves found in Thai curry spice packs and sold in bags in Asian markets. Again, freeze what you don't use immediately and use straight from frozen. The leaves grow in pairs – bruise and use whole, removing before serving, or slice very finely and grind with a mortar and pestle. The word *kaffir* is old Hindi meaning 'foreign'. They are also known as *makrut*.

Vietnamese coriander, often known as *rau rau* and laksa leaf, is fast becoming 'the' Asian

herb. The plants can be bought from nurseries and the cut stems are available from Asian stores. Its refreshing flavour has a hot, citrusy note and the coriander-style pungency stands up well to cooking. It can be added halfway through cooking or wilted in just before serving. You can also scatter it over the dish, to serve.

The long pointed leaf has an aubergine-coloured horseshoe shape in the centre, making it a very attractive addition to the ubiquitous Vietnamese table salads, served with every Vietnamese meal. I also like to deep-fry the leaves.

Its native habitat is on the banks of streams so prefers its roots to be kept moist. Its stems are succulent – a sign of a water-loving plant.

The two most commonly used **Thai sweet basils** are available from Thai and other Asian markets. One has a smooth pale purple stalk with deep green, very sprightly, shiny leaves, squat purple flowers and a strong anise and liquorice aroma and flavour. The other has a brighter green leaf with a tangy, slightly lemony flavour and usually white or pale pink flowers. I have it on good authority that this one is used with fish. The edges of the leaves are smooth on both sweet basils.

Tulsi or holy basil is the sacred herb of Hindu India and believed to be Krishna's favourite plant above any garden flower. It is used as a

religious offering rather than in cooking, although it is used to make a delicious tisane.

There are two types of **Thai holy basil** available in Thai and Asian stores. The most common is the one with pale green, slightly floppy leaves, best wilted into dishes at the last moment when its subtler flavour can come to the fore. When the leaves are squeezed the aroma is very similar to that of engine oil, like a motor mechanic's well oiled overalls. The other holy basil has darker leaves, pinky-purple on the top of the leaf, with deep-pink flowers. The flavour is minty and camphoric and deliciously fragrant when heated. Both these holy basils have a slightly serrated leaf.

Thai mint (*bai sarae nae*) is very fragrant small leafed variety with a hottish taste with a round hairless leaf and, when mature, has a dark red stem. It is often available in Thai stores (only) but it is easy to propagate. Just put a stem into a glass of water until little roots show, then plant it in a pot. This is best done in spring from a bunch bought in a shop with a high turnover. This variety of mint is used quite extensively throughout South-east Asia. I find it perfect in Thai food as its spiciness gives a wonderful dimension to salads.

Vietnamese mint is used as part of the herb collection, 'table salad', which is served with almost every Vietnamese meal, together with coriander and local herbs.

Curry leaf is a musky, spicy, aromatic leaf and not, as its name implies, anything like curry powder, although it is used as a component of Sri Lankan curry powder. These leaves are from a deciduous tree that grows wild in parts of India, Thailand and Sri Lanka.

It's cultivated in southern India where it's popular in many dishes. Here, it is often known as *kari patta* and used as part of a *tarka*, which is a fried mixture that also includes cumin seed, dried chillies and the spice, asafoetida, added to a dish at the end of cooking. Curry leaves are most often used to flavour dishes rather than being eaten, although I chop them into the potato mixture for the Singaras recipe on page 134. I also deep-fry them to sprinkle on top.

Curry leaves are available in all Indian and Asian stores in sealed packs. The thin stalks have about 14 small bright, shiny, green leaves that will keep in the refrigerator quite well for weeks. They freeze well, too.

Epazote is native to the Americas, where it grows so enthusiastically it is viewed almost as a weed. It has a pungent flavour and is often used with beans, due to its reputation as a carminative – the ability to reduce the flatulent effect of beans. Its other title, wormseed, explains its other medicinal use.

Epazote is the important flavour in *papadzutes*, fresh corn tortillas rolled with a filling of hard-boiled eggs and swathed in pumpkin seed sauce, mole verde. I love its odorous pungent hemp-like smell it gives when the leaves are squeezed and find it quite addictive. You can also use it raw in salsas, but because of its pungency I prefer to add it to stews and pulses 15 minutes before the end of cooking. It is also available as a seed so you can grow it yourself.

Japanese shiso or **perilla** is related to the basil and mint family. It is as common in Japan as mint is in the West. There are many varieties some nettle-like and some quite frilly. It has a mild sweet cumin-like aroma and the first taste you get is similar. The afterburn is a minty spicy flavour. I'm passionate about it and want it as much as coriander, now that I have a taste for it.

Its main use in Japan is in sashimi, where it is said to protect against any parasites that may be in the raw fish. Green shiso is also used to make *sushi maki*. The cultivated red shiso is used to colour the umeboshi sour plums and is used to garnish beefsteaks, this is perhaps why it is often called the beefsteak plant, although this may also be due to its deep red colour. The seeds are also sprouted in pots, creating red and green cress-like sprouts, which are great for salads. The leaves and flowering tips make wonderful herb tempura and are also delicious sliced into rice and salads. Shiso is also used in Korean and Vietnamese cuisines.

Pandan or screwpine leaves are used to flavour and wrap food in much of South-east Asia. The long, fresh, green leaves are found in most Asian stores and they keep for weeks if they are wrapped in a bag and stored in the salad drawer of the refrigerator. Bruise the leaves before using as a flavouring. It's quite floral and sweet, ideal for adding to sweet rice dishes, pancakes and curries. I like to use the leaves to wrap fish for steaming or threaded on bamboo sticks with chicken for satays. Extract the juice from the leaves and use it as a bright green food colouring – lovely in dishes such as coconut rice pudding or pancakes.

NOT QUITE A HERB – ALMOST A VEGETABLE

Fenugreek leaves, also known as methi, are native to Asia and south eastern Europe. Buy fresh fenugreek in the vegetable section of Indian and Middle Eastern stores.

The bushy, silvery, olive-green leaves have a nutty pungent sweet curry aroma. It has tightly budded pale ivory flowers and it grows a little like its relative, clover. In Iran where it's a popular ingredient, it goes by the name of *shambaleeleh* or *shambalides* meaning 'clover-like vegetable'. In Lebanese stores it is known as *halbeh*. It is often added to the Iranian *coucou sabzi* recipe on page 49 and to *gormeh sabzi*, a braised lamb dish with kidney beans. In Yemen and Ethiopia it is a staple vegetable.

Fresh bunches of fenugreek will keep happily in a plastic bag in the salad drawer of the refrigerator for up to five days.

Watercress was a highly valued spring energy tonic in ancient Persia. It gives a fabulously intense colour to soups and sauces, when added at the last moment and blended just before serving. Its wonderful hot, peppery flavour is perfect used in pesto-like sauces. Watercress is a favourite vegetable in Chinese cooking – usually briefly cooked in stir-fries or on its own, blanched and tossed with sesame oil.

Sorrel grows like a weed all over Europe and western Asia. The young leaves are tender and flop easily when picked, but refresh very well after 20 minutes in cold water. Don't be fooled by its spinach-like appearance, the flavour is very different, with a distinct astringent lemon taste. The colour is not bright green like spinach. Unless it is used fresh in salads, sorrel will always turn khaki green when cooked.

Sorrel is famously used in soups, especially potato soups, or in salads with sliced tomatoes and good olive oil. Roll a pile of leaves into a big fat cigar and slice thinly. One of the classic uses is in a sauce for salmon, where its acidity cuts the richness of the creamy pink flesh.

CHOOSING, CHOPPING, PRESERVING

Choosing herbs

Herbs are the best value and will have the best flavour if you buy them in big bunches from street markets and farmers' markets.

Herbs bought in small packs or little pots from a supermarket may have been pampered in polytunnels and grown out of their natural season, so check their flavour.

Herbs add their own character of flavour and fragrance on a sliding scale. Some herbs can be quite overpowering if used in a heavy-handed way, so get to know their strength.

The herb's aroma and flavour comes from the volatile oils stored in the leaves, flowers and stems. The time of day they are harvested and the seasons can have a marked effect on their strength. The same herb grown in a variety of conditions can smell and taste quite different.

Woody herbs tend to stand up to longer cooking and can be added at the beginning of cooking. Those with soft leaves are a little more sensitive and are best added towards the end to retain their flavour and goodness.

Chopping and preparing herbs

Herbs give out their individual aroma and flavour when chopped, torn, shredded, bruised, crushed or heated. Useful guidelines are:

• Use a very sharp blade for chopping herbs, so the leaves don't lose all their goodness into your chopping board.
• A mezzaluna is easy to use and ideal for coarsely chopping herbs – it has a curved double-handled blade, which you rock from side to side over the leaves.
• When using a knife, wrap the herbs into a tight bunch with your fingers, then chop with the blade close to your fingers, and angled away from you.
• To chop even finer, bunch the leaves back together again, and chop using the knife as a pivot.
• Chopping leaves in a food processor is fine if you're adding or beginning with other ingredients, otherwise I don't think it's worth it. It's much better to use a large cook's knife. If you need to use this method, use the pulse button to give you more control.
• Chives are easiest snipped into lengths with sharp kitchen scissors, unless you want a very fine finish.
• When using woody herbs or herbs with lots of stalk, strip the leaves off first.
• Herbs such as lemongrass can be bruised to bring out their maximum flavour and used whole or thinly sliced.

• Dry leaves are better to work with, so after washing, drain well and leave on kitchen paper for 20 minutes to air dry. If you don't have time, don't worry – use them anyway. Stronger leaves can be dried in a salad spinner without bruising.

Preserving herbs

Once, dried herbs were almost the only preserved form we knew. Herbs grew in summer and were dried by householders for use throughout the winter and early spring. Some kept their flavour – indeed became stronger – while others faded. Modern farming methods allow us to buy many herbs at almost any time of year, but their flavour will always be different from the ones we remember in the full flush of summer. But they can be preserved in other ways. Cover them with olive oil – blend them with oil, let steep, strain and use the scented oil for cooking. Freeze them and use them straight from frozen. Herbs which benefit from the cold treatment include many tropical ones, such as lemongrass, kaffir lime leaves and curry leaves. If you do use dried herbs, use a small quantity – no more than one-third of that mentioned in the recipe. Some could be left out altogether and another used instead. Use your sense of smell and taste, and be creative.

GROWING YOUR OWN

Growing your own herbs gives the best opportunity for experiment using individual herbs and flavour combinations. Herbs are adaptable plants generous enough to give their all and happy to be picked continually from the garden, a terrace, balcony or inside on a window sill. Providing you don't strip them of all greenery, herbs love to be picked. It makes them bush out and thrive in a very satisfying way. Grow the herb you use most often near the door into your garden, so it can be picked in the rain without you getting too wet. Remember, mint is the number one candidate for container growing as it spreads like wildfire if planted in the ground and left to its own devices.

All plants grow better if their leaves are kept clean, so the kitchen is not the best place to grow herbs. The residue from all that cooking

lands on the leaves and they don't respond well. So it's best to find them a bright window sill away from your cooking.

The content of volatile oil stored in soft leafy herbs increases up to flowering time when the buds have formed but are not quite open. This is when the flavour of soft leaf herbs is at its best. The best time to harvest herbs is before the sun gets too hot and after the early morning dew has dried off the leaves, so morning is good and early evening, too. As soon as they flower, you can prune them right down to get more young growth before autumn. I usually leave my plants to bloom so I can make use of the flowers in cooking and also enjoy their beauty in the garden. The leaves I use will have a greater or lesser flavour over their growing season but that's what I like about

herbs – they never stay the same and they are always available.

I grow herbs among ornamental shrubs and in pots. The majority of herbs adapt well to container life, although watering and feeding has to be fitted into the routine of the day, especially in the summer months. It's best to water your herbs when the sun is off the leaves.

Glazed terracotta pots hold in the moisture for longer so keep the unglazed ones for the herbs that like the sun-baked Mediterranean conditions of a previous life.

Plants whose natural habitat is a dry rocky terrain, like thyme and rosemary, can be grown in smaller pots that may dry out faster. Choose frost-proof terracotta if you intend moving them around because they are lighter than stone. I don't use plastic or lead pots for health reasons.

STARTERS, SOUPS AND SALADS

● **flat leaf parsley**
● **mint (left)**

MINT AND PARSLEY SALAD
turkish ksir

85 g bulghur wheat

2 tomatoes, halved, cored and chopped, with the juices reserved

1 red onion or shallot, finely chopped and soaked in a little lemon juice

½ cucumber, peeled in strips, deseeded and cut into cubes

2 tablespoons extra virgin olive oil

a pinch of cayenne pepper

1 teaspoon ground sumac or the freshly squeezed juice of ½ lemon

a bunch of flat leaf parsley

a bunch of mint

sea salt and freshly ground black pepper

lemon and lime wedges, to serve

serves 2–4

This Turkish salad of bulghur wheat and herbs is similar to the more familiar Lebanese tabbouleh. I like the leaves coarsely chopped, with the mint chopped last, just before serving, so it doesn't turn black. Traditionally, this salad is served with pickled vegetables on boiled vine leaves. I like it served simply with lemon and lime wedges.

Put the bulghur in a bowl and cover with 150 ml cold water. Let stand for about 40 minutes to absorb the liquid.

Put the bulghur in a sieve and squeeze out any excess water. Transfer to a serving bowl, then add the tomatoes and their juices, onion, cucumber, olive oil, cayenne, salt and pepper and half the sumac.

Remove the leaves from the parsley and mint and chop them coarsely. Add to the salad, toss gently and sprinkle with the remaining sumac. Serve with lemon and lime wedges.

Cook's note The reddish-purple sumac berry is a spice tasting a little of lemons. It was used by the Romans before lemons, to do the same job. It is sold ground finely and is available from Middle Eastern stores and spice shops. It's a lovely addition to this salad. If you can't find it, add the freshly squeezed juice of ½ lemon.

● savory (left)

SAVORY FETA SALAD
WITH SUGAR PEAS, EDAMAME AND WATERMELON

200 g edamame (fresh soy beans)

200 g broad beans, shelled

150 g sugar snap peas

½ small watermelon

4 tablespoons sunflower oil

200 g feta cheese

young leaves from 5 sprigs of savory

freshly ground black pepper

serves 6

I grow winter and summer savory in my garden. They are two different plants: summer savory is an annual with tender leaves and softer stalk, while the winter version is an evergreen perennial and is a little stronger and more resinous in flavour. Both are good with beans, including edamame (fresh soy beans). Although the leaves of both summer and winter savory will toughen over the summer, they still retain a wonderful flavour. The spicy peppery taste is at its best in early summer, ready for the first crop of beans. When cut back savagely after flowering, a new crop of tender leaves will appear before autumn.

Bring a large saucepan of unsalted water to the boil. Add the edamame and broad beans and blanch for 2 minutes. Drain and refresh in cold water, then remove the edamame from their pods and the broad beans from their skins. Put into a large serving bowl.

Blanch the sugar snaps in boiling salted water for 30 seconds, drain, refresh under cold running water, drain again, then slice lengthways. Add to the serving bowl with the edamame and broad beans.

Peel and slice the watermelon over a bowl to catch the juices. Cut the watermelon into small wedges, as shown, then add to the salad. Squeeze a few pieces to get about 3 tablespoons of juice in a separate bowl. Whisk the oil into the watermelon juice, then pour over the salad.

Crumble the feta over the top, sprinkle with young savory leaves and pepper, then serve.

- **young flat leaf parsley (left)**
- **chervil**
- **watercress**

OYSTERS ROCKEFELLER

1 shallot, finely chopped

1 small garlic clove, crushed

1 small piece of Florence fennel, finely chopped

75 g unsalted butter

90 ml double cream

3 sprigs of flat leaf parsley

4 sprigs of chervil

4 sprigs of watercress

2 teaspoons Pernod

24 oysters, freshly shucked

a large pinch of cayenne pepper

6 tablespoons fresh breadcrumbs

6 tablespoons freshly grated Parmesan cheese

a grill pan, lined with foil

serves 6

Serve this with champagne as a neat solution for a dinner party starter. The chervil, parsley and watercress are all important to the finished flavour, so do use them all. It's a taste revelation with the chilled oyster holding its own beneath the hot topping. You will notice that chervil not only tastes of anise, but is reminiscent of the liqueur flavour of Pernod. The original recipe was a secret, but I have added cayenne because I have a passion for it. It is just one adaptation that's been made over the years since this dish was first invented in the 1890s in New Orleans.

Put the shallot, garlic, fennel and butter in a frying pan, heat gently and cook until softened and translucent. Add the cream and simmer for 2 minutes. Remove from the heat.

Take the leaves off the sprigs of parsley, chervil and watercress. Chop the leaves and add to the pan, then add the Pernod.

Loosen each oyster from both sides of its shell with a knife and leave it in the deepest shell. Arrange the flat shells on the foil-lined grill pan and balance the round shells on top. Put 1 teaspoon of the herb mixture on top of each oyster.

Put the cayenne, breadcrumbs, Parmesan, salt and pepper in a bowl and stir well. Put 1 teaspoon of the mixture on top of each oyster. Cook under a preheated, very hot grill until just golden, 30–60 seconds, then serve immediately; the idea is not to cook the oysters but to maintain a hot-cold contrast.

BASIL MAYONNAISE
WITH CRISPY PRAWNS

120 g rice stick noodles, broken into 3

24 medium uncooked prawns, shelled, deveined and tail shells intact

2 sheets of nori seaweed, cut into 24 strips

sunflower oil, for deep-frying

mayonnaise

leaves from a large bunch of basil, about 75 g

1 egg yolk

¼ teaspoon salt

1 tablespoon cider vinegar

75 ml olive oil

75 ml sunflower oil

freshly squeezed juice of 1 lime

an electric deep-fryer (optional)

serves 4–6

There is life beyond basil and tomatoes. Basil is wonderful with seafood, and great with mayonnaise. Though spectacular, this dish is not fiddly to make because you can be quite haphazard about it. The noodles frizz up when fried, so all imperfections disappear.

To make the mayonnaise, bring a saucepan of water to the boil, add all the basil and wilt briefly. Drain and run under cold water to cool quickly. Squeeze out as much water as possible and pat the basil dry with kitchen paper.

Put the basil in a blender with the egg yolk, salt, vinegar and 1 tablespoon of oil. Blend to a purée and, with the motor running, gradually pour in the rest of the oils until thick. Spoon into a bowl and add the lime juice to taste.

Fill a wok or deep-fryer one-third full with sunflower oil, or to the manufacturer's recommended level, and heat to 200°C (400°F), or until a piece of noodle will puff up immediately. Bind the lengths of noodle onto the prawns using a strip of the seaweed – dampen the ends of the seaweed and seal together. Add to the hot oil in batches and fry until the noodles puff up and turn slightly golden, about 1 minute. Drain on kitchen paper and trim the ends of the prawns neatly. Serve with the mayonnaise as a dip.

Cook's extra Use the mayo with other things, such as big, homemade chips with masses of fried basil leaves.

- lemongrass
- kaffir lime leaves
- mint or Thai mint
- Thai sweet basil

THAI SPICY SQUID SALAD
yam pla muek

750 g fresh squid tubes, with tentacles

100 g pink Thai shallots

1 stalk of lemongrass, trimmed and thinly sliced

2 long red chillies, deseeded and thinly sliced

3 kaffir lime leaves, rolled up and thinly sliced

2 cm fresh ginger, peeled, thinly sliced, then cut into thin matchsticks

3 spring onions, sliced diagonally

dressing

2 garlic cloves, crushed

2 medium red chillies, finely chopped

freshly squeezed juice of 4 small limes

4 tablespoons Thai fish sauce

to serve

2 tablespoons chopped mint or Thai mint

a handful of Thai sweet basil leaves

serves 6

This spicy Thai squid salad is one of my favourite summer starters, full of light and interesting flavours – all you need to titillate the palate for the dishes to follow. If Thai mint is available, do use it. Though its fragrant leaves look a little ragged, they taste simply fabulous when chopped, adding a hotness that's certainly not to be missed. Thai mint and basil are available in bunches in Asian and South-east Asian markets, and plants are sold in some specialist herb nurseries for you to grow in your garden. Remember they come from a hot climate, so keep them out of the frost.

To make the dressing, pound the garlic and chillies with a mortar and pestle, then add the lime juice and fish sauce. Transfer to a serving bowl and chill until needed.

Cut the squid tubes down one edge to make 1 large piece. Score the inside with a diamond pattern and cut each piece diagonally in half.

Prepare a saucepan of boiling salted water and drop the squid into the water in 2 batches. As soon as they curl up, leave for 1 minute more and drain immediately. Make sure to bring the water back to the boil again before dropping in the next batch. Add the squid to the chilled dressing in the serving bowl while still hot.

Add the shallots, lemongrass, chillies, kaffir lime leaves, ginger and spring onions to the bowl and toss gently. Serve sprinkled with the chopped mint and whole Thai sweet basil leaves.

• shiso (perilla) (left)

SMOKED SALMON TARTARE
WITH SHISO, WASABI JELLY AND SALMON CAVIAR

2 tablespoons agar-agar flakes*

3 tablespoons wasabi paste

150 g smoked salmon, tsar or royal fillet (chunky loin), mildly oak smoked

200 g mouli (daikon or white radish)

100 g jar salmon caviar (keta)

24 shiso leaves

serves 6

Agar-agar, made from seaweed, is available in Asian or health food shops. It is popular in Asia because it sets at 37°C (99°F), so doesn't need to be refrigerated. If using other forms of agar-agar, or for vegetarian gelatine, follow the directions on the packet.

Shiso leaves are the quintessential Japanese herb, sold in little trays in Japanese and Asian markets. It was also popular in England in Victorian times, where it was known as perilla and grown in flower borders, appreciated for its pretty, frilly leaves. I have used the green variety here – there is also a purple shiso, often known as the beefsteak plant because of the colour. To my mind, shiso is sophisticated flavour heaven: the taste is highly aromatic, with warm overtones of sweet anise, coriander and mint. It combines perfectly with rich oily fish.

Put 300 ml cold water in a small saucepan. Sprinkle the agar-agar flakes over the surface and, without stirring, heat to a gentle simmer. When simmering, stir gently for 2–3 minutes. Remove from the heat and add the wasabi, a little at a time, and mix until smooth. Pour into a shallow container, let cool, then refrigerate.

Cut the salmon fillet into small cubes. Cut the jelly into slightly smaller cubes. Peel and slice the mouli into fine matchsticks with a mandolin.

To serve, make little piles of salmon, jelly, mouli, salmon caviar and shiso leaves.

- thyme
- marjoram
- sweet cicely (left)

CHICKEN LIVER MOUSSE

150 g unsalted butter

1 garlic clove, crushed

leaves from 5 sprigs of thyme
or lemon thyme

500 g chicken livers, trimmed

75 ml dry Marsala wine

leaves from 3 sprigs of marjoram

sea salt and freshly ground black pepper

sweet cicely leaves and flowers
or chervil, to serve

1 bowl or 6 small ramekins

serves 6

I like the Italian flavour of Marsala instead of French brandy. The top of the pâté can be decorated with sweet cicely leaves and flowers. If these aren't available, use chervil or fine flat leaf parsley leaves with a few pink peppercorns instead. This is great to take on a picnic, or as a starter for a dinner party – I serve it with toasted wafer-thin slices of walnut bread.

Heat a frying pan over medium heat and add about 15 g butter, the garlic, half the thyme and half the chicken livers. Cook the livers for about 1½ minutes on each side – they should still be slightly pink inside.

Transfer to a food processor and cook the remaining livers and thyme in the same way. Deglaze the pan with the Marsala, then add to the food processor. Add the marjoram, 45 g of the remaining butter and a little salt and pepper.

Blend until smooth, then transfer to a sieve set over a bowl and push the mixture through the sieve with the back of a ladle.

Spoon the resulting mousse into the serving bowl or ramekins and tap on the work surface to settle the mixture. Melt the remaining butter in a small saucepan and pour over the mousse, leaving the sediment in the bottom of the pan. Arrange the sweet cicely and flowers if you have them on top and chill until needed. The mousse will keep for several days in the refrigerator.

- tarragon
- flat leaf parsley
- basil
- marjoram
- Chinese flowering chives (kuchai)

HERB AND CARROT SOUP

3 thin leeks, thinly sliced

2 garlic cloves, crushed

1 tablespoon sunflower oil

600 g young carrots, well scrubbed and thinly sliced

1.2 litres vegetable stock or water

40 g bunch of sorrel, stalks removed and leaves chopped

leaves from 4 sprigs of tarragon

leaves from 6 sprigs of parsley

leaves from 4 sprigs of basil

leaves from 6 sprigs of marjoram

to serve

100 ml crème fraîche

12 bocconcini, torn in half, or 2 regular mozzarella cheeses, torn into pieces

a handful of Chinese flowering chives (kuchai), or regular chives

freshly ground black pepper

serves 6

Aromatherapy in a soup – this dish tastes marvellous, and if you manage to grow all the ingredients yourself, you'll feel wonderfully virtuous. Purée it coarsely, so the brilliant carrot orange is just flecked with green. The bocconcini – little mouthfuls of mozzarella – peep out from just under the surface. Sprinkle with Chinese flowering chives if you have them, otherwise regular chives will taste good, too.

Put the leeks, garlic and oil in a small saucepan, cover with a lid and cook gently for 5 minutes. Add the carrots and cook gently for a further 5 minutes. Add the stock or water, bring to the boil and simmer for 5 minutes. Lower the heat, add the sorrel and simmer, uncovered, for a further 5 minutes.

Coarsely chop the tarragon, parsley, basil and marjoram. Stir into the soup. Strain the mixture through a sieve into a clean pan and put the solids into a food processor or blender with a little of the liquid. Blend to a coarse purée, then return to the pan and reheat.

Remove from the heat and fold in the crème fraîche. Ladle into hot bowls and add a few bocconcini pieces to each one. Sprinkle with chive flowers or regular chives and pepper, then serve.

● **watercress**
● **chervil (left)**

SOUPE VERDON

1 large onion, finely chopped

1 tablespoon sunflower oil

100 g potato, cut into cubes

1 Golden Delicious apple,
peeled and finely chopped

850 ml vegetable or light chicken stock

a large bunch of watercress

a handful of chervil

sea salt and freshly ground white pepper

to serve

double cream or crème fraîche

avruga or other caviar (optional)

serves 4–6

This bright green soup is named after the beautiful river in Provence, north of Brignoles – the green minerals in the rocky bed make the water a wonderful colour. I like it served hot, but it makes a lovely change to have it cold – you will get maximum colour, flavour and goodness if you blend the herbs into the chilled soup.

Put the onion and oil in a saucepan, heat gently, then cook for 5 minutes until softened and translucent. Add the potato and apple, cover with a lid and continue cooking gently for a further 5 minutes. Add the stock and bring to the boil, lower the heat and simmer for 10 minutes. Season with salt and pepper.

Remove any thick or tough stalks from the watercress and remove the chervil stalks (which can taste over-grassy). Chop the watercress and chervil leaves and add to the soup. Simmer for 1 minute, then strain through a sieve into a clean pan. Put the solids from the sieve into a food processor or blender with a little of the liquid and blend to a purée. Return to the pan and reheat gently.

Serve with a swirl of cream or crème fraîche and a spoonful of caviar, if using.

- **kaffir lime leaves**
- **garlic chives (flat Chinese chives)**
- **Thai sweet basil**

THAI LOBSTER NOODLE SOUP

2 small cooked lobsters
or crayfish tails, shells removed

120 g dried shrimp

3 kaffir lime leaves, torn

3 cm fresh ginger, peeled

200 g wide rice noodles (sen lek)

2 tablespoons hijiki seaweed

2 tablespoons mirin (sweetened
Japanese rice wine)

200 ml coconut cream

2 tablespoons fish sauce

freshly squeezed juice of 1 lime

2 mild red chillies, halved lengthways,
deseeded and thinly sliced

2 mild green chillies, deseeded
and thinly sliced

a handful of garlic chives, sliced diagonally

75 g thin green beans, sliced in half
lengthways and cooked

2 sprigs of Thai sweet basil (optional)

serves 4

Like so much Thai food, this recipe has a delicate balance of spicy, fresh, zesty flavours. Kaffir lime leaves are now widely available, either as part of a Thai flavour pack in supermarkets, or in big bags from Asian or Chinatown markets. Buy the whole bag and freeze them, then use straight from frozen. Ginger can also be frozen, then grated from frozen. Both flavours contrast well with the richness of coconut milk and lobster. Seaweed or sesame seeds are my own additions – less Thai than Japanese, but no less delicious for all that.

Put the lobster shells, dried shrimp and kaffir lime leaves in a large saucepan. Add 1.5 litres water and bring to the boil, then lower the heat and simmer for 1 hour. Strain the stock, grate the ginger and squeeze the juice from it into the stock.

Soak the noodles in a bowl of cold water for 20 minutes. When soft, drain well and cover until needed. Put the seaweed in a bowl and stir in the mirin.

Add the coconut cream to the stock, stir well and bring to the boil. Lower the heat, then add fish sauce and lime juice to taste.

When ready to serve, add the drained noodles to the stock and reheat. Ladle into hot bowls, then add the chillies, chives, beans and lobster meat. Drain the seaweed and sprinkle it over the soup, then top with Thai sweet basil leaves and serve.

Cook's extra Fishmongers and Chinese supermarkets often have frozen crayfish tails, which are good for this recipe. Instead of hijiki seaweed, I sometimes use black sesame seeds to sprinkle on top.

BRUNCHES AND LIGHT LUNCHES

- pandanus
- sorrel (left)
- flat leaf parsley

SORREL-SPINACH SOUFFLES
IN PANDAN LEAVES

Sorrel can sometimes be bought in greengrocers, but otherwise grows easily in the garden. When heated, it turns khaki, unlike spinach, which just becomes a more brilliant green. The pandanus leaves used to wrap the soufflés can be found in Asian stores, and give delicate scent and flavour. Don't worry if you can't find them – but if you do discover some, it's always exciting to try new things.

14 pandanus leaves (pandan or screwpine), about ½ metre long (optional)

softened unsalted butter, for greasing

150 ml milk

150 ml double cream

180 g spinach

50 g sorrel

leaves from 4 sprigs of flat leaf parsley, chopped

30 g unsalted butter

30 g plain flour

200 g soft goats' cheese, such as chèvre blanc

4 egg yolks

5 egg whites

sea salt and freshly ground black pepper

4 ramekins, 300 ml each, buttered and chilled

serves 4

If using pandanus leaves, trim both ends to a point. Rub the central 18 cm of 12 of the leaves (shiny side) with butter. Line each ramekin with 3 leaves, buttered side down, so the ends stand upright above the rim of the ramekin.

Cut the remaining 2 pandanus leaves into pieces and put in a saucepan. Add the milk and cream and warm to just below boiling point. Remove from the heat and set aside to infuse.

Plunge the spinach and sorrel into a saucepan of boiling water for 20 seconds, then drain and refresh in cold water. Drain well and squeeze out every drop of water (I squeeze them in muslin). Chop coarsely, add the parsley and reserve.

Melt the butter in a small saucepan, stir in the flour, let cook for 1 minute, then strain in the milk and cream and whisk until thickened. Crumble the cheese into the sauce, add the egg yolks and season well with salt and pepper.

Put the spinach, sorrel, parsley and sauce in a blender and blend to a purée. Transfer the mixture to a bowl. Put the egg whites in a second bowl and whisk until soft peaks form. Fold into the sorrel mixture, a little at first to loosen, then fold in the remainder gently so as not to lose any volume. Carefully spoon the mixture into the ramekins to within 1 cm of the rims. At this point, they can be kept on a tray in the refrigerator for up to 2 hours. When ready to serve, cook on the lowest shelf of a preheated oven at 190°C (375°F) Gas 5 for 25–30 minutes until risen and golden. Remove from the oven and let stand for a few minutes until the sides shrink slightly. Lift the soufflés out of the ramekins using the pandanus leaves, set gently on warm plates and serve immediately.

- chives
- coriander
- oregano
- epazote (left)

GRILLED CHILLI HERB POLENTA
WITH PAPAYA MOJO

a handful of chives

a small bunch of coriander

4 sprigs of oregano

250 g quick-cook polenta

50 g unsalted butter, cut into pieces

50 g Asiago vecchio cheese, freshly grated

2 long red chillies, deseeded and
finely chopped

olive oil spray

sea salt and freshly ground black pepper

papaya mojo

75 g shallots, thinly sliced

grated zest and freshly squeezed juice
of 1 unwaxed lime

5 tablespoons olive oil

1 large papaya, peeled and cut into cubes

a small bunch of coriander

a handful of chives, chopped

sea salt and freshly ground black pepper

epazote beans

100 g black beans, rinsed and drained

2 sprigs of epazote or a pinch of dried

a baking tray or dish, 23 x 32 cm, oiled

serves 6

Epazote is a Mexican herb, available dried and sometimes fresh in Latino markets. It grows like a weed in the garden and it sprouted every year in all my flower pots, until one year it suddenly disappeared. I found I really missed its skunk-like, pungent aroma. Kate, our photographer's assistant, thinks it smells very clean – like bleach. It is famous as a partner for beans, because it counteracts their gaseous tendencies.

To prepare the beans, put them in a bowl, cover with cold water and let soak overnight. Drain, rinse and put them in a saucepan. Cover again with cold water and bring to the boil for 5 minutes. Lower the heat, add the epazote and simmer until just cooked – about 1 hour.

Remove the leaves from the coriander and oregano stalks and chop them coarsely with the chives. Bring 2 pints water to the boil and add a pinch of salt. Add the polenta all at once, whisking constantly. As the polenta thickens, stir in the butter and cheese. Mix well, then fold in the herbs, chillies, salt and pepper.

Pour into the oiled tray, smooth the top with a damp palette knife and let cool. Leave uncovered and chill until 30 minutes before finishing.

To make the mojo, put the shallots and lime juice in a bowl, stir gently, then gradually stir in the oil, papaya, salt and pepper. Remove the coriander leaves from the stalks and chop coarsely, then add to the mojo with the chives. Fold the mojo into the bean mixture.

Carefully take the polenta out of the tray and transfer to a board. Cut into 12 wedges. Heat a ridged stove-top grill pan and, when it starts to smoke, lower the heat a little, spray with olive oil and add the polenta. Grill on the top side for 2 minutes, then turn the pieces 180 degrees to create a criss-cross pattern. Cook for 1 minute more. Serve hot with the papaya mojo and beans.

- **chives or Chinese chives**
- **chervil**
- **tarragon (left)**

BAKED RICOTTA
AND HERB TERRINE

250 g fresh ricotta cheese

4 eggs

1 egg yolk

20 g plain flour

50 g pecorino cheese, grated

½ teaspoon coarsely crushed
dried green peppercorns

a small bunch of chives,
with flowers if possible

a small bunch of chervil

a small bunch of tarragon

to serve

3 tomatoes, preferably an heirloom variety
such as Green Zebra

herb oil

a 500 g loaf tin, greased with butter

*a roasting tin or similar dish,
to hold the loaf tin*

serves 6

I make this terrine in summer with herbs straight from the garden. If chives are in flower, pluck the petals apart and sprinkle them over each serving. Serve with accompaniments such as full-flavoured heirloom tomatoes sold in specialist greengrocers and farmers' markets.

Put the ricotta in a bowl and beat with a wooden spoon until smooth. Beat in the eggs and the extra egg yolk, one at a time. Put the flour, pecorino and pepper in a bowl, stir well, then beat into the ricotta mixture.

Reserve a few chives, then coarsely chop the remaining chives, chervil and tarragon. Fold them into the ricotta. Spoon the mixture into the prepared loaf tin, stand it in a roasting tin and fill with enough water to come halfway up the outside of the loaf tin. (This is called a bain-marie or water bath.) Bake uncovered in a preheated oven at 180°C (350°F) Gas 4 for 35–45 minutes until risen, golden and set.

Remove from loaf tin from the roasting tin (as the terrine cools it will shrink away from the sides). After about 8 minutes, run a knife around the sides of the terrine, then carefully invert it onto a serving dish or board and cut into slices. Cut the tomatoes into wedges. Sprinkle the terrine and tomatoes with the herb oil, add the reserved whole chives and chive flowers, if available, and serve. If serving cold, let cool for at least 15 minutes.

Cook's note Pecorino is a sheep's milk cheese, stronger than Parmesan (which could be used instead).

- parsley
- mint
- oregano
- fennel

HERB OMELETTE WITH PRAWNS
coucou sabzi

6–8 uncooked peeled prawns, tail shells intact

6 large eggs

100 ml milk

5 tablespoons olive oil

1 small bulb of fennel, thinly sliced, then chopped, and a large handful of the green leaves

3 spring onions, thinly sliced

1 young leek, thinly sliced

4 sprigs of parsley

4 sprigs of mint

a small handful of oregano leaves

a large handful of fennel fronds

sea salt and freshly ground black pepper

to serve

crusty bread

crisp green salad

an ovenproof dish, 20 x 27 cm, preferably non-stick, oiled

serves 6

Iran (Persia) boasts one of the world's great cuisines, and *coucou sabzi* (herb omelette) is one of its best-known dishes. I have added chunky prawns to make it a more substantial lunch dish. If you don't have a suitable oven dish, use a frying pan with an ovenproof handle to finish off the cooking. Fennel leaves can be hard to find in stores, because they wilt easily. If you don't grow it yourself, use the green sprouting tops from bulb fennel instead.

To prepare the prawns, devein them, then 'butterfly' them – cut down the back lengthways, but leave the tail fins intact, so they will sit upright when cooked.

Put the eggs and milk in a bowl, add salt and pepper and 2 tablespoons of the olive oil. Whisk briefly.

Put 2 tablespoons of the olive oil in a frying pan, heat gently, then add the chopped fennel and wilt for about 3 minutes. Add the spring onions and leek and stir to wilt a little. Stir into the egg mixture.

Put the leaves of parsley, mint, oregano and half the fennel fronds on a board. Chop them all together, then stir into the eggs. Pour into the prepared ovenproof dish, then sit the prawns upright in the dish.

Cover carefully with foil and cook in a preheated oven at 180°C (350°F) Gas 4 for 25 minutes, then uncover and continue baking until cooked and golden, about 5 minutes more. Tear half the fennel fronds over the top. Set aside for a few minutes before serving.

Cut into wedges, including at least 1 prawn in each piece. Sprinkle with the remaining fennel fronds and serve with crusty bread and a crisp green salad.

- coriander
- Chinese flowering chives (kuchai)

FILIPINO MARINATED FISH SALAD WITH CHIVES
kilaw

3 fillets fine-textured fish with red, pink or silver skins, such as snapper, sea bass or bream, about 750 g

freshly squeezed juice of 2 limes

freshly squeezed juice of 2 lemons

2 pink Thai shallots or 1 regular shallot, halved and thinly sliced

3 cm fresh ginger, peeled and sliced into thin matchsticks

200 ml coconut cream

1 green serrano chilli, deseeded and thinly sliced

1 red serrano chilli, deseeded and thinly sliced

6 spring onions, thinly sliced

a small handful of coriander

6 sprigs of Chinese flowering chives (kuchai)

6 lime wedges, to serve

serves 6

This marinated fish salad from the Philippines uses the same technique of 'cooking' fish in lime juice as the Mexican dish seviche – the acid in the juice changes the texture of the fish and the flesh becomes opaque. Chinese flowering chives, also known as kuchai, are sold in Chinese markets. The leaves are flat, while the flowering stems are round, not hollow, like regular chives. The buds should be closed – if they're open, they're past their best. However, I like to use the flowers to decorate this dish – they have quite a chunky stalk and can be scissored into the dish exactly like chives. If you can't find them, use regular chives and a small crushed garlic clove.

Cut the fish crossways into 5 cm pieces and put in a non-metallic dish. Pour over the lime and lemon juices and sprinkle with the shallots and ginger. Cover with clingfilm and set aside for 4 hours in the refrigerator.

Drain the juices from the fish and mix the juices with the coconut cream. Arrange the fish in a serving dish, pour over the coconut cream mixture and top with the chillies, spring onions, coriander leaves and Chinese flowering chives. Serve the lime wedges separately.

DILL-MARINATED SALMON
WITH PANCAKES AND SABAYON

This traditionally cured salmon takes 36–48 hours to cure and the flavour of the dill penetrates right into the fish. I use a whole fillet of salmon for a party, but if you want it for a smaller group, just halve the recipe. My neighbour, Ireen, is Dutch and she lends me a special pan, called a poffertjes pan, with 19 indentations in it so the little pancakes can be cooked in large batches. Instead, you can use a doughnut pan, such as aebleskiver or blini pan, or make tiny ones, a few at a time, in a regular crêpe pan. A flavoured sabayon is served instead of the usual dill and mustard sauce.

1 kg salmon fillet

2 tablespoons gin

a large bunch of dill

5 tablespoons sea salt flakes

3 tablespoons caster sugar

pancakes

125 g self-raising flour

a pinch of salt

¼ teaspoon baking powder

1 egg

1 teaspoon Dijon mustard

180 ml milk

1 tablespoon freshly chopped dill leaves

sunflower oil, for cooking

sabayon

2 egg yolks

1 tablespoon thin honey

2 tablespoons Dijon mustard

3 tablespoons gin

a poffertjes or aebleskiver pan, blini pan or crêpe pan

serves 6–8:
makes about 36 pancakes

Put the fish on a board flesh side up and rub with the gin. Remove the dill fronds from the thick stalks, chop them, then mix with the salt and sugar and rub into the flesh. Put in a non-metallic dish and cover with clingfilm. Put a board on top with weights on top of that (2 heavy food cans are suitable). Chill for 36–48 hours. Slice thinly at a 45-degree angle to serve.

To make the pancake batter, sift the flour, salt and baking powder into a bowl. Make a hollow in the middle, add the egg, mustard and half the milk. Whisk gently, then slowly add the rest of the milk to make a smooth batter. Add the chopped dill and whisk into the mixture.

Lightly oil the chosen pan. Heat the pan and fill each indentation with batter almost to the top. Fry them until their undersides are brown, then flip them and cook the other side. Keep warm while the remaining batter is cooked.

Just before serving, make the sabayon sauce. Put the egg yolks, honey, mustard and gin in a bowl set over a saucepan of barely simmering water so the bowl doesn't touch the water. Using a hand-held electric beater, whisk until the volume has increased and the mixture foaming and holding its shape.

Serve the pancakes topped with a slice of salmon and a spoonful of sabayon.

A MEAL IN A PAN

300 g medium new potatoes

2 tablespoons olive oil

25 g salted butter

125 g smoked salmon

a small bunch of dill
(strip the feathery leaves
from any very thick stalks)

2 eggs

sea salt and freshly ground pink
or black pepper

*2 small frying pans, about
14 cm diameter, or 1 medium pan*

serves 2

The delicate fern-like glamour of dill is best when fresh, with upright, bright green fronds and umbrellas of pin-like bright yellow flowers. Dill and fennel are famous digestive aids, and are often added to dishes perceived as very rich or fatty, or difficult-to-digest ingredients such as pickled cucumbers or cabbage. In this recipe, dill contrasts with the richness of smoked salmon and egg.

Put the potatoes in a large saucepan, add cold water to cover, bring to the boil, add a large pinch of salt and cook until tender. Drain, then when cool enough to handle, peel or not, as you wish. Slice into 5 mm rounds.

Heat the pan or pans. Add 1 tablespoon of oil and a piece of butter to each pan. As soon as it sizzles, add the sliced potatoes. Fry on both sides over medium heat until golden.

Divide the smoked salmon between the pans, folding it over the potatoes. Tear the dill over the top and break an egg into the centre of each pan. Add the pepper, cover with a plate or lid and cook over low heat for 3 minutes until the egg has just set. Serve immediately.

Cook's extra Scallops can be used instead of the salmon. Slice crossways into discs and fry briefly. If quails' eggs are available, use 2 per serving instead of 1 hen's egg.

- **young flat leaf parsley (left)**
- **bay leaves**
- **thyme**

PARSLEYED HAM
jambon persillé

This Burgundian Easter classic requires lots of very fresh flat leaf parsley and a beautiful piece of cured ham, plus some jelly-making ingredients and a large pinch of commitment!

1 kg best-quality cured pork or ham steak (gammon), soaked overnight

1 medium veal knuckle, chopped into pieces

1 shallot

2 carrots

¼ teaspoon black peppercorns

a large bunch of flat leaf parsley

2 bay leaves

a large sprig of thyme

4 sheets of leaf gelatine or 2½ tablespoons powder (optional)

150 ml white wine

1 tablespoon tarragon vinegar

3 egg whites and shells

to serve

crusty bread

radishes

gherkins

serves 6–8

Put the pork or ham, veal, shallot, carrots and peppercorns in a large saucepan. Strip the leaves off the parsley and put them in a plastic bag in the refrigerator. Tie up the parsley stalks, bay leaves and thyme with string to make a bouquet garni and add to the pan. Cover with water and heat to a gentle simmer with the water hardly moving. Cook for about 1½ hours or until very tender.

Lift the ham out onto a plate and let cool. When cold, cover and store in the refrigerator. Simmer the liquid for another 30 minutes. Lift out the knuckle and strain the liquid through a sieve into a bowl and let cool. When cool, measure 750 ml and put it in the refrigerator overnight (keep the rest for soup).

If it has set to a firm jelly, there will be no need to use the gelatine (otherwise soak and use the gelatine after clarifying the liquid). If it has not set, use a baster to extract liquid from the centre, leaving the fat behind. If it has set, skim off any fat and spoon the jelly into a pan. Heat until just melted. Add the wine and vinegar.

Put the egg whites and shells in a bowl and whisk well. Add to the pan and, whisking constantly, gradually bring to the boil. As soon as the froth rises to the top of the pan, stop whisking and take it off the heat. Let settle for 4 minutes.

Take care that the crust on top does not break, then heat the liquid once again just to the boil. As soon as it rises, take off the heat and leave for 10 minutes.

Meanwhile cut the gammon into small pieces and discard any fat. Gently strain the liquid through a sieve set over a bowl lined with a double thickness of muslin. Cool to a point where it has almost set to jelly. Chop the reserved parsley leaves and add to the jelly. Then add the ham. Spoon into a glass bowl right to the top (or use several small bowls), then let set in the refrigerator. Serve with crusty bread, radishes and gherkins.

- kaffir lime leaves
- Thai holy basil

THAI BEEF CURRY WITH BASIL
pha naeng neua

750 g beef fillet

400 ml coconut milk

1–2 tablespoons red Thai curry paste

85 g peanuts, roasted and ground

2 tablespoons palm sugar

5 kaffir lime leaves

3 tablespoons Thai fish sauce

a bunch of Thai holy basil

freshly squeezed juice of ½ lime,
or to taste

to serve

2 teaspoons sunflower oil

150 g beansprouts,
rinsed, trimmed and drained

8 pink Thai shallots or 2 regular shallots,
thinly sliced

2 mild green chillies, deseeded and
sliced into rings (optional)

serves 6

There are two kinds of Thai holy basil – the one with dark purple-tinged leaves, stalk and flower is the most fragrant when heated in curries and this is the variety used in meat curries. The leaves are more sturdy and, when you crush them between your fingers, they have a minty, almost camphor-like aroma. The lighter, paler, Thai holy basil has a softer, slightly hairy leaf with a distinct oily aroma. It is used in non-meat curries and noodle dishes. If you can't find either of these, sprinkle Thai sweet basil over the dish at the last moment.

Cut the beef in half lengthways, then into thin diagonal slices. Put half the coconut milk and the red curry paste in a wok and heat slowly until just boiling. Add the rest of the milk and simmer gently for 5 minutes. Add the peanuts, palm sugar and kaffir lime leaves and simmer for a further 2 minutes. Strip the leaves from the holy basil and add to the wok, then add the fish sauce. Stir in the beef and cook for 1 minute to wilt the basil leaves and lightly cook the beef. Add lime juice to taste and serve in 6 deep bowls.

Heat the oil in a wok, add the beansprouts and stir-fry for 1 minute. Add to the bowls of curry, top with the shallots and chillies, if using, and serve immediately.

Cook's extra To deseed a chilli before slicing into rings, massage it between your thumb and forefinger until the seeds feel loose inside. Cut off the stalk end and bang the chilli on the work surface so all the seeds fall out. To cut into fine matchsticks, cut in half lengthways and remove the seeds with a teaspoon. Slice thinly.

MAIN COURSES

fennel (left)

FISH IN A FENNEL SALT CRUST

2 lemons

1 kg snapper or sea bream, scaled and cleaned

plenty of fennel stalks, foliage and flowers

250 g grey sea salt

250 g sea salt flakes

serves 2

I grow two kinds of fennel in my garden – regular and bronze. It's a pretty herb to grow, but if you don't have any, use the tops from a bulb of Florence fennel. However, in this recipe I like to use the whole plant – stalks, foliage and flowers. The salt forms a crust which keeps the fish moist. It does not make the fish very salty, because the crust is removed before serving, but it does somehow enhance the flavour of the sea.

Cut 1 lemon into slices and use to stuff the cavity of the fish. Reserve a handful of fennel, and stuff the rest into the cavity.

Put the grey salt and salt flakes in a bowl and mix well. Put half the mixture in an ovenproof dish and shake to level. Arrange the fish in a single layer, then pack the remaining salt over the fish. Insert the remaining fennel into the salt.

Bake in a preheated oven at 200°C (400°F) Gas 6 for 15–20 minutes or until cooked. To test, insert a skewer through the salt into the fish – if it comes out very hot, the fish is done.

Crack open the crust and remove most of the salt. Serve with the remaining lemon cut into wedges.

Cook's extra Serve with a simple salsa of tomato, parsley and onions all chopped finely and mixed with olive oil.

- coriander
- mint

FISH WITH CORIANDER AND MINT WRAPPED IN LEAVES
patra ni macchi

6 skinless fish fillets, such as cod, about 175 g each

freshly squeezed juice of 1 lime, plus 1 lime, cut into wedges, to serve

sea salt

6 patra leaves or 6 pieces of banana leaf or foil, about 22 cm square

coriander mint chutney

75 g desiccated coconut

3 garlic cloves, crushed

3 large green chillies, deseeded and finely chopped

a large bunch of coriander

a large bunch of mint

½ teaspoon caster sugar

½ teaspoon ground coriander

freshly squeezed juice of 1 lime

sea salt

raffia or string, to tie the parcels

a baking dish with a rack

serves 6

Real chutney, in India, is fresh, and quite unlike the British versions. This one is flavoured with spices as well as coriander and mint and is bright green, in terrific contrast to the white flesh of the fish. Patra, traditionally used to wrap the fish, is taro leaf, sold in Asian markets. If you can't find it, use banana leaves instead – or just foil. Either way, the parcel is unwrapped before eating – you don't eat the wrapper.

Put the fish on a plate. Mix the lime juice with the salt and rub into the fish. Cover and set aside in a cool place.

To make the chutney, put the coconut, garlic, chillies, coriander leaves, mint, sugar, ground coriander, lime juice and a small pinch of salt in a food processor and pulse to a coarse paste.

Use the paste to coat the topside and underside of the fish, then wrap in leaves or foil and tie with raffia or string.

Put the fish parcels on a rack in a baking dish with a little boiling water in the bottom. Cover with a foil tent and cook in a preheated oven at 220°C (425°F) Gas 7 for about 15–20 minutes. Discard the banana or patra leaves or foil and serve immediately.

- **flat leaf parsley**
- **coriander**

HAKE IN GREEN SAUCE

12 mussels

16 clams

90 ml cava sparkling wine

4 hake steaks cut through the bone, about 200 g each (leave the bone in)

150 ml olive oil

4 garlic cloves, thinly sliced

1 tablespoon finely chopped flat leaf parsley, plus sprigs to serve

1 tablespoon finely chopped coriander leaves

sea salt

serves 4

Hake is a favourite fish in Spain, where I discovered this dish. It is becoming seriously overfished, so feel free to substitute other white fish, such as cod, ling or haddock. As it cooks, the fish gives out white juices, which you shake to form an emulsion with the oil. Wine and chopped herbs turn this emulsion into a wonderfully delicious green sauce. This dish is usually cooked in a flameproof earthenware cazuela, a flat cooking dish that retains heat well. I find a heavy enamelled non-stick frying pan is equally good.

Put the mussels, clams and wine in a saucepan over high heat. As the shellfish open, remove them to a bowl and cover with clingfilm. Discard any that fail to open. Strain the cooking juices through a muslin-lined sieve and set aside.

Put the hake on a plate and sprinkle with a little salt 10 minutes before cooking.

Put the oil and garlic in a heavy-based frying pan and heat gently so the garlic turns golden slowly and doesn't burn. Remove the garlic with a slotted spoon and keep until ready to serve.

Pour about two-thirds of the oil into a jug and add the hake to the oil left in the pan. Cook over very low heat moving the pan in a circular motion – keep taking it off the heat so it doesn't cook too quickly (the idea is to encourage the oozing of the juices instead of letting them fry and burn). Add the remaining oil little by little as you move the pan, so an emulsion starts to form. When all the oil has been added, remove the fish to a plate and keep it warm. Put the pan on the heat, add the reserved clam juices and stir to form the sauce.

Return the fish to the pan, add the chopped parsley and coriander and continue to cook until the fish is cooked, about 5 minutes. Just before serving, add the opened mussels, clams and fried garlic to the pan to heat through.

- lemongrass
- kaffir lime leaves
- Vietnamese coriander or laksa leaf (left)

FRIED BREAM THAI-STYLE

This idea is based on a dish I found in a tiny eatery on a remote island in Thailand. It had just three tables and food was cooked on burners set on the ground behind a rush screen. Lunch was whatever the ocean had to offer that day. The view was spiritually uplifting and the food was divine. I could no more live without the classic Thai ingredients – lemongrass and kaffir lime leaf – than garlic and onions. The lime leaf's Thai name is *makrut* – 'kaffir' is the Hindi word for a foreigner, perhaps reflecting the odd way the leaves grow in pairs. They are waxy and smooth, in contrast to the fruit, which has knobbly skin. Both leaf and zest have a wonderfully fragrant lime flavour.

8 red bream or snapper fillets, about 750 g

3 tablespoons sunflower oil

3 red chillies, deseeded and thinly sliced

2 stalks of lemongrass, trimmed and thinly sliced

8 pink Thai shallots or 2 regular shallots, thinly sliced

5 cm fresh ginger, peeled, thinly sliced and cut into matchstick strips

6 kaffir lime leaves, rolled and thinly sliced

12–18 Vietnamese coriander (laksa leaves)

oil, for frying

6 limes, cut into wedges, to serve

marinade

2 garlic cloves, finely chopped

2 stalks of lemongrass, trimmed and thinly sliced

1 teaspoon coriander seeds

1 teaspoon Szechuan pepper

1 teaspoon finely ground star anise

1 teaspoon ground galangal (Laos powder)

½ teaspoon salt

½ teaspoon freshly ground black pepper

serves 4

Cut each fillet in half and slash each piece twice on the skin side.

To make the marinade, use a mortar and pestle to grind the garlic, lemongrass, coriander seeds, Szechuan pepper, star anise, galangal, salt and pepper to a fine paste. Rub the paste into the slashes and into the flesh side of the fish pieces, then let marinate for 30 minutes.

Meanwhile, fill a wok about one-third full with oil, heat to about 190°C (375°F), or until a piece of noodle will puff up immediately. Add the chillies, lemongrass, shallots, ginger and lime leaves and deep-fry until crispy – work in batches if necessary to ensure a crisp result. Remove from the wok and drain on kitchen paper. Deep-fry the Vietnamese coriander in the same way – the leaves are left whole and are fragile when crisp. Remove from the wok and drain on kitchen paper. Pour the oil into a heatproof container and let cool.

To cook the fish, wipe any excess marinade off the skin side. Put about 100 ml of the oil back into the wok and heat gently. Working in batches, fry the fish, flesh side down over medium heat, for 1 minute, then turn the pieces over and fry for 1 minute more. As each piece is cooked, remove from the wok and pile onto plates. Serve topped with the crispy lemongrass mixture, deep-fried Vietnamese coriander and lime wedges.

- celery leaves
- flat leaf parsley
- chervil

CRISP-FRIED HERBED HALIBUT
WITH SHOESTRING POTATOES

750 g waxy potatoes,
such as Belle de Fontenay

1 egg white

1 tablespoon milk

750 g halibut fillet, cut into 8 pieces

3 sprigs of chervil

3 sprigs of flat leaf parsley

100 g plain flour

1 teaspoon black sesame seeds

½ teaspoon chilli powder

sea salt and freshly ground white pepper

sunflower oil, for deep-frying

to serve

celery leaves

flat leaf parsley leaves

spicy ketchup, for dipping

an electric deep-fryer

serves 4

Celery leaf makes a delicious herb, and plants are now available in pots from garden centres. You could also use the pale leaves growing inside an ordinary head of celery. Celery and flat leaf parsley leaves are perfect crisply fried and curly parsley is also good. Chervil and parsley are used to flavour the coating on the fish.

Using a mandolin, cut the potatoes as thinly as possible into strips, then put into a bowl of cold water to rinse off the starch. Drain and dry well with kitchen paper.

Fill a deep-fryer with oil to the manufacturer's recommended level and heat to 180°C (350°F). Working in batches, fry the potatoes until golden, then drain on kitchen paper. Keep hot.

Put the egg white and milk in a bowl and mix well. Rub the fish pieces with the egg white mixture. Finely chop the leaves from the chervil and parsley.

Sift the flour into a bowl, then add the chopped chervil and parsley, the sesame seeds, chilli powder, salt and pepper.

Deep-fry the celery and parsley leaves – they spit like mad, but will be crisp as soon as the spitting stops. Remove and drain on kitchen paper. Dip the fish into the bowl of flour mixture to coat, and fry 2 pieces at a time for 2–3 minutes until just cooked. Drain on kitchen paper and serve with the fried leaves, ketchup and crisp shoestring potatoes.

- chives (left)
- wild garlic (ramsons)

SEA BASS WITH CHIVE CREAM

4–8 sea bass fillets

salt

oil, for brushing (optional)

chive cream

70 g unsalted butter, cut into pieces

2 thin banana shallots or 4 regular shallots, finely chopped

125 ml white wine

125 ml double cream

a handful of chives

4 wild garlic leaves (optional)

sea salt and freshly ground black pepper

to serve (optional)

caviar

wild garlic flowers

Chinese bamboo steamers

serves 4

An elegant dinner party dish; serve two fillets for a main course or one as a fish course. The caviar is an indulgence which you can choose to have – or have not! Everyone should grow chives in a patch in the garden or in a pot on the terrace or window sill, partly because you can harvest the pinky purple pincushion flowers anytime for salads or sprinkling over dishes but mainly because it's so nice to grab a handful of spiky leaves to snip over buttery new potatoes or mashed potatoes. If you have access to wild garlic (ramsons), a few flowers will add a stylish look and the leaves add extra flavour.

To make the chive cream, put 30 g of the butter in a frying pan, add the shallots and cook for 3 minutes without colouring. Add the wine and cook until reduced by two-thirds. Add the cream and bring to the boil, remove from the heat, then whisk in the remaining butter and add salt and pepper to taste.

Brush the grids of the steamers with oil, or line with 3 of the garlic leaves to prevent the fish from sticking. Sprinkle the flesh side of the sea bass with a little salt and fold in half with the skin on the outside. Steam in Chinese steamers over simmering water for about 2 minutes. Check to make sure the fish is still folded – if not, press down with a spoon and continue steaming for a further 2 minutes until just cooked (remember the fish will carry on cooking in its own heat so don't overdo the cooking).

When the fish is almost done, chop the chives and one of the garlic leaves, if using. Put in a blender, pour in the cream and shallot mixture and purée until smooth. Reheat very gently without boiling. Put 1–2 pieces of fish on each plate, with the sauce under or over it. Top with a spoonful of caviar and wild garlic flowers, if using, and serve.

- coriander
- fenugreek leaves

CORIANDER CHICKEN WITH FENUGREEK
murgh methi

6 skinless, boneless chicken thighs

1 teaspoon cumin seeds, freshly ground

4 tablespoons sunflower oil

1 onion, finely chopped

5 garlic cloves, crushed

5 cm piece of fresh ginger, grated

4 green chillies, deseeded and chopped, plus extra for serving

½ teaspoon ground turmeric

2 teaspoons coriander seeds, freshly ground

½ teaspoon fenugreek seeds, toasted in a dry frying pan, then ground

400 ml coconut milk

leaves from a bunch of fenugreek (methi), about 30 g, or a pinch of ground fenugreek

leaves from a bunch of fresh coriander, about 30 g, plus extra sprigs, to serve

50 g roasted slivered almonds, toasted in a dry frying pan

sea salt and freshly ground black pepper

Indian breads, such as pooris, or rice, to serve

a large flameproof casserole

serves 4

The seeds of the fenugreek or methi plant are a common Indian spice. The leaves of the plant are sold in Indian and Middle Eastern greengrocers, and the spice seeds in the spice section of many supermarkets. In fact, they are what gives curry powder its distinctive aroma. In my opinion, nothing compares with the astringently aromatic flavour of the fresh leaves and, if you have a garden, it's definitely worth growing yourself. However, when you buy the leaves, make sure they are fresh and perky – don't keep them too long in water, because the leaves will lose their flavour. If you can't buy fresh fenugreek, this recipe is also good with just fresh coriander leaves and the fenugreek seed.

Cut the chicken into large pieces, season with salt, pepper and ground cumin and set aside for 15 minutes at room temperature to develop the flavours.

Heat 2 tablespoons of the oil in a flameproof casserole, add the chicken pieces and fry until golden. Using a slotted spoon, remove to a plate. Heat the remaining oil in the casserole, add the garlic and fry until softened and translucent, about 7 minutes. Add the garlic, ginger and chillies, increase the heat and add the turmeric, coriander and fenugreek seeds. Stir in 250 ml of the coconut milk and heat to simmering. Return the chicken pieces to the casserole and cover with the lid. Cook in a preheated oven at 190°C (375°F) Gas 5 for 20 minutes.

Put the fenugreek leaves and coriander in a blender, add the remaining coconut milk and blend to a purée. Add to the chicken and cook for a further 5–10 minutes. Top with coriander sprigs, almonds and extra chilli, if using, and serve with Indian pooris or rice.

BREAST OF GUINEA FOWL
STUFFED WITH HYSSOP
AND GOATS' CHEESE

1 tablespoon olive oil

4 guinea fowl breasts, with wing bone only left in and skin on

150 g firm goats' cheese, rind removed

4 sprigs of hyssop or lemon thyme

2 tablespoons thick honey

6 teaspoons orange flower water or rosewater

sea salt and freshly ground black pepper

mixed soft leaf herbs and flower salad, to serve

a shallow ovenproof dish

serves 4

Hyssop is still used today in Bedouin cooking. A native of the Mediterranean it comes with pink or blue flowers which, like all herb flowers, are pretty in salads and for sprinkling over other dishes. It has a sweet anise flavour with slightly minty undertones. It can be quite pungent depending on the time of year, so just add a little at a time to see how you like it. No hyssop? Try using one of the thymes, perhaps lemon or orange scented thyme.

Heat the olive oil in a large frying pan, add the guinea fowl skin side down and sear the skin until golden. Remove from the pan and carefully cut a pocket in each breast to contain the filling.

To make the filling, put the cheese and hyssop or thyme in a bowl. Add 1 tablespoon of the honey, 2 teaspoons of the orange flower water, salt and pepper and mash well. Use to stuff the pockets in the breasts.

Arrange the breasts in the ovenproof dish. Mix the remaining orange flower water with 75 ml water and pour over the breasts. Poach in a preheated oven at 200°C (400°F) Gas 6 for 25 minutes until cooked.

Remove from the oven, put the breasts on a plate and cover with foil. Keep in a warm place for 8 minutes. Transfer the juices to a small saucepan and reduce over medium heat until reduced by one-third. Stir in the remaining honey to make a syrup.

To serve, cut the breasts diagonally, then serve on warm plates, trickle the syrup over the top and serve with a pretty herb and flower salad.

- basil
- coriander

RICH LAMB STEW
WITH BASIL AND CORIANDER

4 tablespoons olive oil

750 g lamb neck fillets or boneless leg of lamb, cut into 2 cm chunks

2 large onions, chopped

2 garlic cloves, crushed

2 sweet red ramiro peppers, deseeded and chopped

4 ripe tomatoes, skinned, deseeded and coarsely chopped

½ teaspoon cayenne pepper

250 ml fresh vegetable stock or water

10 prunes

10 dried apricots

100 g okra, trimmed

2 Granny Smith apples, peeled, cored and cubed

400 g canned chickpeas, drained and rinsed

1 pomegranate, cut in half

a bunch of basil

a bunch of coriander

sea salt and freshly ground black pepper

a large ovenproof casserole

serves 6–8

This is my version of *bozbash*, an Armenian rich lamb stew, packed with herbs and fruity delicious flavours and textures. Neck fillet cooks quickly to tenderness due to the small amount of fat running through it, so I use it in preference. Pomegranates are a typical ingredient in this part of the world – sweet yet tart, with glorious colour, but leave them out if they're not in season. Potatoes are usually cooked in the stew, but I prefer a baked potato with lots of butter melting in its open top, giving a contrast in texture. The herbs must be added at the last moment to keep their aromatic freshness.

Heat a large ovenproof casserole over high heat, add 2 tablespoons of the oil, then add the lamb in batches and brown on all sides. Remove to a plate, add 1 tablespoon of oil to the casserole, add the onions, garlic and red peppers and fry gently over low heat for 10 minutes.

Increase the heat and add the tomatoes and cayenne and cook until bubbling, about 5 minutes. Add the browned lamb, the stock or water, salt and pepper and bring to a gentle simmer. Cover with a lid and cook in a preheated oven at 200°C (400°F) Gas 6 for 20–30 minutes until just softening. Add the prunes and apricots and cook for a further 10 minutes.

Heat the remaining 1 tablespoon of oil in a frying pan, add the okra and apple and fry for 5 minutes. Transfer the okra, apple and chickpeas to the casserole and cook for 10 minutes. Test the meat for tenderness. If not yet done, lower the oven to 180°C (350°F) Gas 4 and cook for a further 10 minutes. Just before serving, squeeze the juice from half the pomegranate and fold into the casserole. Coarsely chop the herbs and fold half into the stew. Serve sprinkled with the remaining herbs and the seeds from the remaining pomegranate half.

LEG OF LAMB STUFFED WITH DATES, HERBS AND SPICES

6 tablespoons extra virgin olive oil

2 onions, finely chopped

a large pinch of saffron threads

4 garlic cloves, 2 crushed, 2 sliced

12 lavender or rosemary leaves, chopped, plus extra flower sprigs, to serve

¼ teaspoon ground cinnamon

1 teaspoon ground cumin

2 tablespoons pine nuts, toasted

10 mozafati or medjool dates, pitted and coarsely chopped

1.5 kg leg of lamb (about 1.15 kg after boning)

sea salt and freshly ground black pepper

a roasting tin with a rack

serves 6

You can buy legs of lamb part-boned, with the shank end of the leg left in and the thighbone removed to leave a pocket for the stuffing. If you can't find one, ask the butcher to do it for you, or do it yourself. Ask for it to be tunnel-boned rather than butterflied. Take note of the weight of the meat, so you will know how long to cook it. The stuffing is flavoured with the strong aromas of lavender or rosemary. I add extra sprigs to the lamb for the last 5 minutes to flavour the outside. The strength of the herb depends on the time of year – the leaves of spring and early summer will be milder than in high summer, when the volatile oils are at their strongest from the heat of the sun.

To make the stuffing, heat 5 tablespoons of the oil in a frying pan, add the onions, saffron and crushed garlic and fry until soft and golden. Add the chopped lavender or rosemary, the cinnamon, cumin, pine nuts, dates, salt and pepper and mix well. Remove from the heat and let cool. If time allows, prepare it ahead and keep in the refrigerator to mature the flavours.

Push the stuffing into the boned section of the meat. Secure closed with skewers (or sew up with string). If the meat has been in the refrigerator, let it come back to room temperature. Set on a rack in a roasting tin and add about 250 ml water to the tin. With the point of a knife, cut tiny pockets in the skin, push in the sliced garlic, then season the skin well with salt and pepper.

Cook in a preheated oven at 200°C (400°F) Gas 6 for 20 minutes, then lower the heat to 180°C (350°F) Gas 4 and cook for a further 15 minutes for each 500 g of lamb. Top up with a few teaspoons of water if it dries out to stop the bits burning on the pan. Five minutes before the end, tuck the flower sprigs into the holes in the skin. Remove from the oven and let it rest on a warm serving dish for 15 minutes before slicing, to serve. Check with a meat thermometer if you have one – the internal temperature should be about 60°C (140°F).

- coriander
- bay leaves (left)

PORTUGUESE PORK AND CLAMS WITH BAY LEAVES

750 g pork shoulder steaks

150 ml extra virgin olive oil

about ¼ teaspoon sea salt

1 onion, finely chopped

100 ml white wine

500 g potatoes, cut into 1.5 cm cubes

a handful of coriander leaves, plus extra sprigs to serve

500 g fresh manila or venus clams, in the shell

sea salt and freshly ground black pepper

lemon wedges, to serve (optional)

marinade

2 tablespoons red sweet pepper cream (*crema di pepperoni*)*

1 tablespoon sweet paprika

1 chilli, deseeded and finely chopped

2 whole cloves

2 fresh bay leaves

5 garlic cloves, crushed

a large flameproof casserole

serves 4

*available from good delicatessens

Pork and clams – *carne de porco a Alentejana* – make a simple meal from southern Portugal, a region where bay, coriander and garlic richly flavour the dishes. Apart from Portugal and parts of Spain, coriander isn't a traditional herb in European cooking. Prepare this dish in advance, then steam open the clams and add herbs before serving.

To make the marinade, put the pepper cream, paprika, chilli, cloves, bay leaves and garlic in a glass or ceramic bowl. Cut the pork into large chunks and add to the bowl, then add 4 tablespoons of the oil and mix to coat the meat. Let marinate for 2 hours or overnight in the refrigerator.

Thirty minutes before cooking, remove the pork from the refrigerator and sprinkle it with the salt. When ready to cook, heat 1 tablespoon of the oil in a flameproof casserole, add the onion and fry for 7 minutes until softened but not coloured. Remove to a plate. Add 2 tablespoons more oil, then sear the meat in batches on both sides over high heat. As each is browned, transfer to a plate using a slotted spoon. Increase the heat, add the wine and boil hard for 30 seconds. Add the pork, salt and pepper, cover with a lid and cook in a preheated oven at 180°C (350°F) Gas 4 for 40 minutes. Remove the lid and cook, uncovered, for a further 5 minutes.

Just before serving, heat the remaining oil in a large frying pan, add the potatoes and fry until tender and golden on all sides. Keep them warm until ready to serve. Chop the coriander leaves.

Put the clams in a saucepan with about 3 tablespoons of water. Cover with a lid, bring to the boil and cook until the clams open, about 3–4 minutes. Discard any that don't open. Remove the clams from the pan and strain the juices through a muslin-lined sieve set over a bowl. Add the juices to the casserole, then stir in the chopped coriander. Add the opened clams, potatoes and sprigs of coriander to the casserole and serve with lemon wedges, if using.

- lemongrass
- coriander

PORK WITH LEMONGRASS, GINGER AND CHILLIES

1.3 kg piece of boneless pork belly

½ teaspoon ground star anise

½ teaspoon ground Szechuan pepper

¼ teaspoon sea salt

1 tablespoon sunflower oil

8 banana shallots, thinly sliced, about 8 oz.

5 cm fresh ginger, peeled and thinly sliced

4 garlic cloves, thinly sliced

2 stalks of lemongrass, split lengthways and bruised

1 large red chilli, deseeded and finely chopped

to serve

1 tablespoon sunflower oil

a bunch of spring onions, sliced diagonally

about 400 ml cooked jasmine rice

6 sprigs of coriander

a casserole just big enough to hold the pork

serves 4–6

The clean citrus flavour of lemongrass and Chinese spices really permeates the flesh of the pork. Slow cooking is perfect for pork belly: it has a high fat content and cooks to a texture that cuts like butter, perfect hot or cold. The skin can be removed after cooking and crisped like crackling. After lengthy covered cooking, the skin is very soft and can be scored in a fine diamond pattern ready for crisping. Alternatively, the skin can be removed before cooking.

Rub the underside of the pork with the star anise, Szechuan pepper and salt. Put the oil, shallots, ginger, garlic, lemongrass and chilli in a casserole just big enough to fit the piece of pork. Stir well, then put the pork on top. Cover with a lid and cook in a preheated oven at 180°C (350°F) Gas 4 for 20 minutes. Lower the oven temperature to 150°C (300°F) Gas 2 and cook for a further 1 hour 40 minutes.

Slice the pork into bite-sized pieces. Heat a wok over medium heat, add the oil and the spring onions and stir-fry for 30 seconds. Add the pork, the contents of the casserole and the cooked jasmine rice to the wok and stir-fry until heated through. Add the coriander and serve.

Cook's extra Alternatively, if cooking the pork with the skin on, score the skin with a sharp knife after 1 hour 10 minutes and cook uncovered for a further 30 minutes. Remove the skin and crisp it on a tray under the grill for about 3 minutes. Serve the belly and skin cut into squares with the bits from underneath. Serve with a vegetable stir-fry or bok choy.

SAGE AND POTATO GRATIN
WITH BACON AND ONIONS

1 kg medium salad potatoes, peeled

30 g unsalted butter

1 small onion, halved and thinly sliced

300 ml double cream

400 g smoked rindless streaky bacon

12–18 sage leaves

sea salt and freshly ground black pepper

a large deep baking dish, greased with butter

serves 4–6

Matahami, the French dish of layered bacon, potato, onions and herbs, is traditionally made with thyme and green bacon, but I prefer it with sage and smoked bacon. It was the first dish I mastered in domestic science lessons and I carried it home with pride in a Red Riding Hood-style basket. Salvia, the generic name for sage, is from the latin word *salvere*, which means 'to be in good health'. I grow many varieties, ranging from a variegated leaf, *Salvia officinalis* 'Tricolor' to the purple-leaved *Salvia officinalis* 'Purpurascens', but my favourite is the moleskin leaf of the Greek sage, *Salvia fruticosa*.

Put the potatoes in a saucepan of cold water, bring to the boil and add salt to the water. Cook for 12 minutes or until you can just pierce them with a skewer (they should be not quite cooked). Drain the potatoes well and slice as thinly as possible.

Heat half the butter in a frying pan, add the onion and cook until softened and translucent, about 5 minutes.

Put the cream in a saucepan, bring to the boil and simmer for 3 minutes. Arrange one-third of the bacon in the prepared baking dish. Put 4 sage leaves on top. Add a layer of half the potato slices, then another of half the onion. Pour in half the cream. Put half the remaining bacon on top and 4 more sage leaves. Use the remaining potatoes and onion in the same way, pour in the remaining cream, then put the remaining bacon and sage on top.

Dot the sage with the remaining butter, then bake in a preheated oven at 200°C (400°F) Gas 6 for 20 minutes. Cover the dish with foil and bake for a further 30 minutes. Using a skewer, test to see if the potatoes are soft all the way through. If necessary, return to the oven, uncovered, for a further 5–10 minutes, making sure that the bacon and sage don't burn.

- oregano (left)
- purple or opal basil

BASIL AND OREGANO SALSA WITH CHAR-GRILLED STEAK
chimichurri

6 thick sirloin steaks, about 1.5 kg total

sea salt and freshly ground black pepper

oil, for brushing

chimichurri

1 small shallot, chopped

3 garlic cloves, crushed

6 sprigs of oregano

a large bunch of purple basil

1 stalk of fresh green peppercorns,
or 1 tablespoon green peppercorns
preserved in brine

150 ml olive oil

1 tablespoon red wine vinegar

1 red chilli, deseeded and finely chopped

to serve

watercress

sprigs of purple basil

serves 6

This Argentinian pesto-like salsa is usually made with parsley and is served in individual small bowls with thick, rare, char-grilled steaks. I have a big bowl of peppery fresh watercress to serve with it. Purple or 'opal' basil has a minty, oil of cloves quality to its flavour. The purple-black leaves become brighter and more intense in colour when plunged into hand-hot water – this will also revive a flopped bunch within 10 minutes. Oregano is widely used in Latin American cuisine.

Using a mortar and pestle, pound the shallot and garlic to a coarse paste.

Pull the leaves off the sprigs of oregano and basil and pound into the paste. Remove the peppercorns from the stalk and pound them into the paste. Start adding the oil a little at a time, then pound in the vinegar and chilli, keeping the mixture chunky.

Brush the steaks with oil and season well. Heat a ridged stove-top grill pan and, when it starts to smoke, add the steaks and cook for about 1½–2 minutes on each side. Remove them and let rest in a warm place for 5 minutes. Slice thickly and serve with the chimichurri, watercress and basil sprigs.

Cook's note It is traditional to use a mortar and pestle to make the chimichurri. However, use a blender to save time if you prefer, pulsing to keep the paste as coarse as possible.

VEGETABLES

- parsley
- marjoram (left)

IMAM BAYILDI

4 large aubergines, with long stalks if possible, halved lengthways

200 ml extra virgin olive oil

500 g onions, halved and very thinly sliced

4 garlic cloves, crushed

750 g Italian plum tomatoes, skinned, deseeded and finely chopped

leaves from 15 sprigs of flat leaf parsley

leaves from 12 sprigs of marjoram

2 teaspoons sugar

1 small lemon, thinly sliced

sea salt and freshly ground black pepper

an ovenproof dish, big enough to hold the aubergines in a single layer

serves 4–8

Over the years, I have eaten many versions of this Middle Eastern aubergine dish. Some have been meltingly delicious, others not so nice. The dish got its name because the priest (the Imam) found it so delicious that he swooned. Some stories tell that he really fainted because he was horrified at the amount of oil used to cook it. This is the secret of course – aubergines must be cooked well, with large quantities of oil. So this, for my palate, is the definitive recipe for an ancient dish. It uses the heavily scented marjoram – when it has its knotted flowers in bloom, use those, too – and lots of parsley.

Cut a line 5 mm in from the edges of the aubergine halves, then score the flesh inside with a criss-cross pattern. Rub plenty of oil all over the aubergines and season with a little salt. Arrange in a single layer in the ovenproof dish. Cook in a preheated oven at 200°C (400°F) Gas 6 for about 30 minutes or until the flesh has just softened.

Heat 75 ml of the oil in a heavy-based frying pan, add the onions and garlic, cover with a lid and cook over low heat until soft. Increase the heat and add the tomatoes. Cook until the juices from the tomatoes have reduced a little, then add salt and pepper to taste. Reserve a few parsley leaves for serving, then chop the remainder together with the marjoram. Add to the onion and tomato mixture, then add the sugar.

Scoop some of the central flesh out of the aubergines, leaving a shell around the outside to hold the base in shape. Chop the scooped out section and add to the tomato mixture. Pile the mixture into the aubergine shells and sprinkle with pepper. Arrange the lemon slices on top. Trail more oil generously over the top, then sprinkle with 4 tablespoons of water.

Cover with foil and bake for 30–40 minutes until meltingly soft. Remove the foil about 10 minutes before the end. Serve, sprinkled with any remaining oil and the reserved parsley.

SAGE BUTTERED BABY LEEKS
WITH CHILLI BREADCRUMBS

75 g salted butter

2 tablespoons finely chopped sage

500 g short thin baby leeks,
split halfway through and well washed

2 tablespoons extra virgin olive oil

50 g fresh ciabatta breadcrumbs

1 mild long red chilli, deseeded
and finely chopped

1 smaller red chilli, deseeded and
sliced into rings

serves 4

Sage makes a great partnership with leeks, and the Italian-style chilli breadcrumb topping makes a delicious combination. For an even more pronounced Italian accent, the crispy crumbs are made from ciabatta bread. If possible, use the mild, tender leaves of the gold variegated sage, *Salvia officinalis* 'Icterina', for a less 'thuggish' medicinal flavour.

Put the butter and sage in a bowl and mash well.

Steam or boil the leeks for about 5 minutes, or until tender. Toss in half the sage butter and keep hot.

Heat a frying pan, add the oil and ciabatta breadcrumbs and fry for about 45 seconds. Add the remaining sage butter and all the finely chopped chillies. Fry until golden.

Put the leeks on a serving plate, and top with the chilli breadcrumbs and the smaller sliced chilli. Serve with other dishes or as a starter.

Cook's extra Sea kale and salsify are also good served this way.

- lovage (left)
- thyme

ARTICHOKES PROVENÇAL

1 lemon, halved

18–24 baby artichokes, depending on size

3 tablespoons extra virgin olive oil

200 g smoked bacon pieces (lardons)

300 g small shallots

3 garlic cloves, halved

4 carrots, halved lengthways and cut into fine strips

200 ml white wine

100 ml vegetable stock

2 young sprigs of lovage, or a few celery leaves

a large sprig of thyme

200 g cooked flageolet or cannellini beans

sea salt and freshly ground black pepper

to serve

crusty bread

boiled red Camargue rice

salad leaves

a heavy, shallow flameproof casserole

serves 6

Based on a Provençal dish, baby artichokes are picked before the hairy choke has formed. I use lovage, thyme and beans in this recipe, cooked in a shallow terracotta dish. Lovage grows well – its strong green leaves push up through the soil in April and will grow as tall as my garden fence if left unused, so I keep it trimmed to ensure a good supply of new leaves. Only a small amount of lovage is needed to give maximum flavour. If you've never tasted it, prepare to be smitten – it's a delightful herb, full of character, similar to celery in some ways.

Squeeze the cut lemon halves into a bowl of cold water and add the lemon shells. Set aside to add the artichokes as they are prepared (the acidulated water will prevent them from discolouring).

To prepare the artichokes, remove about 3 layers of tough leaves from the outside, cut off the top 1 cm of the leaves and trim the stalks to about 3 cm. Using a vegetable peeler, peel the stalks. As you work, add the artichokes to the bowl of lemon water.

Heat 1 tablespoon of oil in the casserole, add the bacon and fry until crisp and golden. Transfer to a plate.

Add the remaining oil to the casserole, then fry the whole shallots and garlic until golden. Drain the artichokes and add to the pan. Add the carrots and stir-fry for 2 minutes. Add the wine, bring to the boil and reduce for 2 minutes. Add the stock and simmer for 2 minutes, then add the lovage, thyme, salt and pepper.

Cover and cook in a preheated oven at 200°C (400°F) Gas 6 for 20 minutes until the artichokes are tender. Add the beans, return to the oven and heat through, uncovered, for 5 minutes. Serve with bread, boiled rice and salad.

• rosemary
• bay leaves (left)

OVEN-ROASTED VEGETABLES,
WITH ROSEMARY, BAY LEAVES AND GARLIC

500 g ratte or other salad potatoes, cut into 5 cm chunks

about 500 g butternut squash, cut into wedges and deseeded

6 small red onions, quartered

4 tablespoons extra virgin olive oil

8 garlic cloves, unpeeled

2 red romano (long) peppers, deseeded and cut into chunks

4 sprigs of rosemary

4 sprigs of bay leaves

sea salt

a large baking tin

serves 4

Roasted vegetables are made extra special with the strong flavours of herbs. Thyme is good, but I love rosemary (be sparing though – too much can overwhelm a dish). Bay leaves are quite mild when young, so don't use as many if you have mature leaves.

Bring a large saucepan of water to the boil, add salt and the potatoes and cook for 5 minutes. Drain, then put in a large baking tin. Add the squash, onions and 2 tablespoons of the oil. Toss to coat, then roast in a preheated oven at 200°C (400°F) Gas 6 for 10 minutes.

Add 1 extra tablespoon of oil to the baking tin, followed by the garlic and peppers, 2 sprigs of rosemary and 2 sprigs of bay leaves. Roast for 15 minutes, then add the rest of the herbs and continue roasting for 10–15 minutes. Turn the vegetables occasionally until they are all tender and the edges slightly charred. Trail the remaining oil over the top, then serve.

Cook's extra Sprinkle with 3 tablespoons of pine nuts and some crumbled feta cheese 5 minutes before the end of the cooking time, so the nuts roast a little and the feta softens.

PASTA, RICE AND BREAD

- chervil
- flat leaf parsley
- sweet cicely

HOMEMADE HERB PASTA
WITH HERB OIL

200 g Italian typo '00' pasta flour
or plain flour*

2 large eggs (orange yolks will give a
stronger pasta colour)

about 36 fresh herb leaves, such as chervil,
flat leaf parsley, sweet cicely, or flowers such
as marigolds and nasturtiums (make sure
they aren't damp), plus extra to serve

a small bag of baby spinach, about 200 g

3 mild dried chillies, deseeded and
ground with a pinch of salt

sea salt

homemade herb oil, such as basil
or parsley, to serve (page 138)

a pasta machine

serves 4

*Pasta dough made with typo '00' pasta flour
can be made 1 day ahead and kept
refrigerated. Ordinary plain flour dough turns
grey after 3 hours if left uncooked.

Homemade herb pasta is fun to make with your children – it's almost like paper making. There is no limit to the fun they can have dashing out to the garden to see if this leaf or that petal will suit. I found that it's a good way to teach children what they can eat from the garden.

Put the flour and a pinch of salt in a food processor and pulse to mix. Put the eggs in a bowl and beat with a fork, then add to the food processor. Pulse until the mixture forms fine balls (like couscous), then transfer to a work surface. Knead to form a ball, then wrap in clingfilm and chill for 1 hour.

Cut the dough into 3 pieces and wrap each one in clingfilm. Set the pasta machine to the widest setting. Working with one piece of dough at a time, roll out once, then fold it into 3 layers. Repeat 4 times, no matter how crumbly, in order to achieve a pliable dough.

Gradually narrow the settings, rolling twice through each setting, then put it through the narrowest setting 3 times. Cover the sheet of dough with clingfilm, then fold into 3, so it is interleaved with clingfilm. Make sure it is well sealed with clingfilm to stop it drying out. When all the dough has been rolled out, cut one sheet crossways into 7 cm wide strips and cover with clingfilm.

Take one strip of pasta and put a herb leaf at one end. Fold over the other end to cover the leaf evenly. Roll twice through the machine on the second narrowest setting to stretch the leaf trapped in the pasta sandwich. Trim any rough sides, but any odd shapes are fine. Repeat with the remaining dough.

Bring a large saucepan of water to the boil, add 2 teaspoons of salt and cook the pasta in 2 batches for 1 minute each. Add half the spinach with each batch, just before draining, and drain immediately so the spinach is just wilted. Put in warm pasta bowls and sprinkle with the chilli salt mixture and a few marigold petals, if you have them. Trail the green herb oil over the top and serve immediately.

PURPLE BASIL RAVIOLI
WITH TRUFFLE BUTTER

Purple basil, which adds a hint of minty spice to the potato stuffing, is also known as opal basil. The one with a ruffled leaf has an interesting liquorice flavour, but is less easy to find unless you grow it yourself. This dish is worth the effort for a special dinner and can be made the day before.

a large pinch of saffron threads

2 large eggs

200 g Italian typo '00' pasta flour

500 g purple-fleshed potatoes, such as Blue Congo

50 g Manchego cheese, finely grated

8 sprigs of purple basil

1 egg white

sea salt

truffle oil, to serve

truffle butter

50 g jar black truffles

60 g unsalted butter, cut into pieces

a pasta machine

5 cm fluted ravioli cutter

serves 4–6, makes 36 ravioli

Note I prefer to freeze the ravioli and cook from frozen, which stops them sticking together.

To make the pasta dough, use a mortar and pestle to grind the saffron to a fine powder with a little salt. Add the eggs one at a time and mix thoroughly. Put the flour in a food processor and pulse for a second, then add the egg mixture. Pulse until the mixture forms fine balls (like couscous), then transfer to a work surface. Knead to form a ball, then wrap in clingfilm and chill for 1 hour.

Meanwhile, put the potatoes in a saucepan and cover with cold water. Bring to the boil, add salt and cook until the potatoes are very soft. Drain and, when cool enough to handle, peel off the skins. Mash and let cool, then stir in the Manchego. Pull the leaves off the sprigs of basil, chop and add to the potato mixture.

Cut the pasta dough into 3 pieces and wrap each one in clingfilm. Set the pasta machine to the widest setting. Working with one piece of dough at a time, roll out once, then fold it into 3 layers. Repeat 4 times, no matter how crumbly, in order to achieve a pliable dough. Gradually narrow the settings, rolling twice through each setting, then put it through the narrowest setting 3 times until you have a long thin sheet. Cover the sheet of dough with clingfilm, then fold into 3, so it is interleaved with clingfilm. Make sure it is well sealed with clingfilm to stop it drying out. When all the dough has been rolled out, cut each sheet into 12 strips, 7 cm wide. Cover with clingfilm.

Put 1 teaspoon of potato mixture on one end of a strip of dough and brush egg white around it. Fold the dough strip over and seal it, expelling any air as you work. Stamp out around the filling using the ravioli cutter. Use a little extra flour if the dough is too soft.

To cook the pasta, bring a large saucepan of lightly salted water to the boil. Add the pasta and cook for 2–3 minutes. Drain, reserving 150 ml cooking water.

To make the truffle butter, slice one large truffle thinly and chop the rest. Put the chopped truffles in a blender with the butter and reserved cooking water and blend. Pour the truffle butter over the pasta, toss gently, then serve topped with the sliced truffle and a few drops of truffle oil.

- borage
- flat leaf parsley
- lemon geranium

FRESH HERB RISOTTO

800 ml light vegetable stock

100 g unsalted butter

2 tablespoons extra virgin olive oil

2 red onions, finely chopped

300 g risotto rice, such as arborio

100 ml white wine

a handful of borage leaves

350 g yellow courgettes,
.cut into 1 cm cubes

250 g fine or wild asparagus

a handful of flat leaf parsley leaves

a few lemon geranium leaves (optional)

100 g wild rocket

sea salt and freshly ground black pepper

to serve

80 g fresh Parmesan cheese shavings

a few borage flowers (optional)

serves 4–6

I love this risotto for its summer quality – using up all those yellow courgettes. Lemon geranium leaves go into it to give a citrus tang and borage leaves to give a cucumber flavour. I use borage instead of spinach and prefer the young leaves – I also make use of the flowers to scatter over the dish. Take care when picking borage – the leaves are a bit furry and can produce a rash. Use gloves if you're sensitive. The only one to eat (leaves and flowers) is *Borago officinalis*. It gave Roman soldiers courage, although I can't imagine a tough legionary chewing on a blue star-shaped flower.

Put the stock in a saucepan, bring to the boil, then keep over very low heat.

Put half the butter and all the oil in a heavy-based frying pan and heat until the butter melts. Add the onions and cook until translucent but not coloured.

Stir in the rice and turn to coat in the hot oil. Increase the heat and add the wine, which will splutter and eventually be absorbed. Add half the borage leaves, then stir in 1 ladle of hot stock.

Add the courgettes and asparagus. Coarsely chop the parsley leaves. Add 1 tablespoon of the parsley and the lemon geranium leaves, if using, then another ladle of stock. Keep adding the stock as it is absorbed.

When the rice is cooked, but still *al dente*, add the remaining borage leaves and butter, rocket, parsley, and salt and pepper to taste. Remove and discard the lemon geranium leaves.

Serve, topped with Parmesan shavings and borage flowers, if you have them.

Cook's note Because borage and lemon geraniums are only available to people who grow them in their own gardens, they can be replaced with 4 cm piece of cucumber (instead of borage) and the finely peeled zest of 1 lemon (instead of lemon geranium). Remove both before serving.

RICE AND LENTILS WITH HERBS
bhooni kitcheri

250 g whole red lentils (masoor dhaal)

250 g basmati rice

80 g unsalted butter

12 curry leaves or 3 bay leaves

2 cm fresh ginger, peeled and grated

2 garlic cloves, crushed

½ teaspoon chilli powder

sunflower oil, for frying

10 banana shallots or regular shallots, about 400 g, thinly sliced

a large bunch of coriander, coarsely chopped

3 fresh green chillies, deseeded and finely chopped

sea salt and freshly ground black pepper

to serve

4 hard-boiled eggs, quartered

2 lemons, cut into wedges

a heat diffuser

serves 6

The Indian *kitcheri*, meaning 'a bit of a mess' or a porridge, was the precursor to the British colonial dish of kedgeree. The *bhooni* part of the title means the porridge is dry not wet. Fragrant curry leaves are sold in Indian greengrocers, but if unavailable, use bay leaves or a kaffir lime leaf. This is a wonderful dish, and if you want to give it a flavour of the Raj, add poached smoked haddock before serving. Any whole lentils can be used, but beware of Puy lentils, which will turn the rice a grey colour. I find whole red lentils from Indian stores taste best, but Italian brown lentils are excellent, too. There is a large quantity of coriander in this dish, but it's very good – don't skimp.

Put the lentils in a bowl, cover with cold water and let soak for 30 minutes. Put the rice in a sieve or colander and wash under cold running water until the water runs clear. Drain the lentils and rice.

Put the butter in a large saucepan and heat until melted. Add the drained lentils and rice and stir to coat with butter. Add 4 of the curry leaves or all the bay leaves, the ginger, garlic, chilli powder, salt and pepper. Cover with 850 ml cold water, stir and bring to the boil. As soon as it boils, cover with a lid and lower the heat to low (use a heat diffuser). Cook for 30 minutes.

Meanwhile, heat the oil in a frying pan, add the remaining curry leaves, if using, and fry for 10 seconds. Remove and drain on kitchen paper – the leaves crisp as they cool. Add the shallots in 2 batches and fry until crisp and golden. As they are ready, remove and drain on kitchen paper.

When the kitcheri is ready, fluff it up with a fork and fold through the coriander and two-thirds of the fried shallots and all the chopped chillies.

To serve, fluff up the rice with a fork and top with the fried curry leaves, if using, the remaining fried shallots, hard-boiled eggs and lemon wedges.

● sage

SAGE SCHIACCIATA BREAD
WITH CHEESE AND ONION

350 g unbleached bread flour

½ teaspoon salt, plus extra to serve

7 g fast-acting dried yeast (1 tablespoon)

2 tablespoons olive oil, plus extra to serve

4 large sage leaves, coarsely chopped

3 tablespoons olive oil, plus extra to serve

cheese and onion topping

30 g Manchego cheese, grated

1 red onion or 4 pink Thai shallots, sliced into rings

8 sage leaves, chopped

freshly ground black pepper

a baking tray, dusted with flour

serves 6–8

The Italian word *schiacciata* means 'flattened', which is how this focaccia-style bread gets its name. This version is flavoured with sage, which has always been seen as a healthy herb, famous for its antiseptic qualities. It can have a very strong, medicinal flavour, so it should be used sparingly.

Put the flour, salt and yeast in a large bowl and mix well. Put the oil in a measuring jug, add 250 ml hand-hot water and stir well. Make a hollow in the flour and pour in the liquid. Mix with your hand and, when it all comes together, transfer to a floured work surface. Knead for 5 minutes until the dough is elastic. Put the dough in an oiled bowl, cover and let rise in a warm place for 1 hour.

Transfer the dough to a work surface, add the sage and knead for 2–3 minutes. Put the dough on a baking sheet and shape it into a flat circle about 22 cm diameter, then make indentations over the surface of the dough with your fingers. Brush with the 3 tablespoons of olive oil and leave at room temperature for 10 minutes.

Cook in a preheated oven at 200°C (400°F) Gas 6 for 10 minutes. Remove from the oven, spread the grated cheese on top, followed by the onion rings, freshly ground black pepper and chopped sage leaves. Cook for a further 10 minutes, then increase the heat to 220°C (425°F) Gas 7 and cook for another 5 minutes or until cooked. To test, insert a skewer in the middle. It should come out clean – if it doesn't, cook for 5 minutes longer.

Sprinkle with sea salt flakes and more olive oil, then serve.

● rosemary

PISSALADIÈRE

Pissaladière is the Provençal version of pizza. I like to cook the onion topping in white wine and extra virgin olive oil – the tastes are intense, so they need a challenging sister flavour, such as the highly aromatic, pine-like qualities of rosemary. Though it isn't traditional, I like to add roasted red pepper for a hint of colour.

275 g plain flour

2 teaspoons fast-acting dried yeast

½ teaspoon salt

1 egg, beaten

1 tablespoon extra virgin olive oil

topping

1 kg white onions, thinly sliced

2 tablespoons brown caster sugar

125 ml extra virgin olive oil

150 ml white wine

1 sprig of rosemary and 2 tablespoons chopped rosemary leaves

1 large ramiro pepper

2 teaspoons anchovy paste

100 g canned anchovies, drained and halved lengthways

about 20 black olives

freshly ground black pepper

a baking tray, about 30 x 25 cm

serves 6–8

To make the dough, put the flour, yeast and salt in a large bowl and mix briefly. Put the egg and oil in a small bowl, add 150 ml hand-hot water and whisk well. Make a hollow in the flour and pour in the egg mixture. Using your hand, mix until the dough comes together into a ball. Transfer to a floured work surface and knead for about 5 minutes until soft and elastic. Transfer the dough to an oiled bowl, cover with clingfilm and let rise in a warm place for 1 hour.

To make the topping, put the onions in a large, heavy-based saucepan. Stir in the sugar, 60 ml of the oil, the wine and a sprig of rosemary. Cook over low heat for 30 minutes, turning every 10 minutes so the onions don't burn. The liquid should evaporate leaving the onions soft and deliciously perfumed.

Using a toasting fork or tongs, hold the red pepper over a gas flame and char until blackened all over. Put into a plastic bag and let steam for 10 minutes to soften. Rub off the skin under cold, running water, then remove the seeds and slice the flesh into thin lengths. Set aside.

Transfer the dough to a floured work surface and knead for 1 minute. Roll out to a rough rectangle, then put into the baking tray, pushing the dough to the edges and fitting it into the corners. Mix the anchovy paste with 2 tablespoons of the oil and smooth onto the dough base. Brush the edges with more oil. Remove the sprig of rosemary from the onions and stir in the chopped rosemary. Pour the mixture over the dough. Arrange the anchovies and pepper strips side by side in a diamond pattern and leave for 10 minutes at room temperature. Bake in a preheated oven at 190°C (375°F) Gas 5 for about 20 minutes. Remove from the oven, put the olives in the centre of each diamond, pour over the remaining oil, sprinkle with pepper and return to the oven for a further 5 minutes (cover with foil if over-browning). Serve warm or at room temperature.

SWEET THINGS

● **kaffir lime leaves (left)**

SUMMER FRUIT SALAD
WITH KAFFIR LIME SORBET

40 g kaffir lime leaves

225 g caster sugar

150 ml white wine, such as pinot grigio

1 egg white

1 orange-fleshed melon, such as Charentais
or cantaloupe, halved and deseeded

1 green-fleshed melon, such as honeydew,
halved and deseeded

1 small watermelon,
preferably seedless, halved

2 ripe mangoes, cheeks removed

4 large kiwifruit, peeled

1 dragon fruit, peeled

*an ice cream maker
or freezer-proof container*

melon ballers

serves 4–6

**Dragon fruit is a large pink tropical fruit
covered with green and yellow horns. Its
flesh is sweet, with tiny black seeds like
vanilla. It is sold in Chinese and Asian
markets, and sometimes in up-market
greengrocers and supermarkets.
If unavailable, omit or use another
tropical fruit, such as papaya.*

Use any fruit that you can scoop out with a melon baller for this salad. Kaffir lime leaf, with its clean citrus flavours, is used to perfume the syrup. Pour the syrup over the fruit and churn the remainder into a soft sorbet. It seems like a lot of leaves, but it works. Buy them in big bags from Chinese or Asian markets, then use them fresh or freeze and use straight from frozen. Any leftovers may be used to make Thai curries. They grow in pairs, as shown.

Tear the lime leaves and arrange in layers in a saucepan, sprinkling the sugar between the layers. Set aside for several hours or overnight to develop the flavours. Add 250 ml water and slowly heat to dissolve the sugar. Boil for 1 minute and transfer to a bowl to chill.

Strain the syrup and measure 200 ml into a bowl. Add the wine and 100 ml water and chill in the refrigerator. Set the remainder aside until you are ready to make the salad.

Add the egg white to the chilled syrup and wine and whisk just to break it up. Transfer to an ice cream maker and churn according to the manufacturer's instructions. Eat immediately or store in the freezer. Alternatively, put the mixture into a large freezer-proof container and freeze, stirring occasionally to break up the ice crystals.

When ready to serve, scoop balls of fruit into a bowl using one or several sizes of melon ballers. Pour the reserved syrup over the top and keep cool until needed. Serve with scoops of sorbet.

LEMONGRASS-GINGER SYRUP
WITH DRAGON'S EYES

250 g caster sugar

2 cm piece of fresh ginger, peeled and thinly sliced

3 stalks of lemongrass, bruised and coarsely chopped

2 starfruit (carambola)

36 fresh longans or lychees, peeled and deseeded, or 2 cans, about 560 g each, drained

finely grated zest and juice of 1 unwaxed lime

2 baking sheets, lined with silicone baking parchment

serves 6

'Dragon's eyes' is the romantic name for the longan fruit, a relative of the lychee, which you can use instead, either fresh or canned, though I prefer canned. Longans, which look like huge bunches of brown hairy grapes, are only available fresh in autumn, and you'll see special vendors selling them in Asian markets. Lemongrass and ginger are the distinctive flavours of Thailand. They make an easy syrup for this simple pudding to finish a Thai-style dinner and, like other Asian ingredients, are easy to use from frozen.

Put the sugar and 350 ml water in a heavy-based saucepan and heat gently to dissolve. Increase the heat, add the ginger and lemongrass and boil for 8 minutes until syrupy but still pale. Remove the pan from the heat and let cool completely.

To make the starfruit crisps, peel off the brown ridges of the starfruit with a vegetable peeler. Slice the fruit crossways very thinly using a mandoline. Arrange them on kitchen paper. Brush the top side with a little of the cold syrup and set them on the prepared baking sheets, painted side down. Lightly brush the top side with syrup. Transfer to a preheated oven and cook at 110°C (225°F) Gas ¼. Gently turn them over after 30 minutes, return to the oven and dry them out for a further 15 minutes. Carefully peel off the paper.

Strain the syrup, leaving in a few bits of ginger. Add the longans, lime juice and zest to the cold syrup and chill until ready to serve with the crisps.

Cook's extra To test if the starfruit crisps are ready, take one out, it should crisp as it cools. They can be kept stored in an airtight container until ready to use. Apples can be cooked in the same way (there's no need to core or peel them).

- **tansy or bay leaves**
- **viola**

TANSY PANNA COTTA

a medium bunch of fresh young tansy leaves, sweet cicely or 6 bay leaves

600 ml double cream

40 g caster sugar

75 g white chocolate drops

3 sheets leaf gelatine or 1 sachet powdered gelatine

crystallized flowers (optional)

1 egg white

a large handful of violas (heartsease) or violets

caster sugar (see method)

6 ramekins or moulds, 100 ml each

a heat diffuser

serves 6

Tansy is an old-fashioned herb, which is now available in all garden centres, and is very useful in the garden as a pest controller. A perennial, it grows to a fine height and has bright yellow, button-like flowers, and was used in Victorian nosegays. If unavailable, use sweet cicely or flavour the cream with 6 bay leaves.

To crystallize the flowers, put the egg white in a bowl and whisk lightly to break it up. Paint the flowers lightly with the egg white, then put the caster sugar in a tea strainer and sprinkle it all over the flowers. Transfer to parchment paper and leave in a warm, dry place until crisp. They will keep in an airtight container for about 1 week.

To prepare the panna cotta, strip the fern-like young tansy leaves from the centre stem or the sweet cicely leaves in the same way. Purée in a blender with 60 ml of water and the same of cream. Pour through a nylon sieve set over a bowl and press out the juice with a ladle and reserve (discard the pulp).

Put the remaining cream in a saucepan and heat gently over low heat to just below boiling point (use a heat diffuser so it takes about 15 minutes). Add the sugar and chocolate and mix to dissolve. Soften the gelatine in cold water for 10 minutes and add to the pan and stir to dissolve. Cool for 20 minutes. Add the tansy or sweet cicely juice and stir well.

Arrange the ramekins on a tray, pour in the mixture, cover and chill to set. To serve, unmould the panna cottas by dipping the bases in hot water, invert onto plates, top with the crystallized heartsease and violets, if using.

rose-scented geranium (left)

ROSE MERINGUETTES
WITH ROSE GERANIUM SYRUP

12 rose-scented geranium leaves

160 g caster sugar

1 teaspoon red cake sugar crystals
(from the baking section of the supermarket
or specialist suppliers)

2 large egg whites

a pinch of cream of tartar

crystallized leaves and petals*

petals from 4 small rosebuds

a handful of rose geranium flowers

small leaves from the top of rose
geranium sprigs

1 egg white

caster sugar (see method)

chantilly cream

300 ml double cream

2 teaspoons sifted icing sugar

1 teaspoon rosewater

2 baking sheets, lined with baking parchment

makes 12

**Ensure the leaves and petals have not been
sprayed with anything harmful.*

These meringues have rose-scented sugar as their base. Scented geraniums are available in garden centres – ask for *Pelargonium capitatum* (rose-scented geranium) or the variety Attar of Roses. It is the leaves, rather than the flowers, which have the strongest scent. Native to South Africa, these plants have been popular since the 17th century. For the best scent, let the sugar sit with the leaves for 4 days. Alternatively, just use a few extra drops of rose water in the mixture, mixture or strongly scented unsprayed rose petals.

To crystallize the leaves and petals, follow the method on the previous page.

To scent the sugar, put the geranium leaves and sugar in an airtight jar and set aside for 4 days. When ready to make the meringues, remove the leaves from the sugar and discard the leaves. Put 60 g of the scented sugar into a clean electric coffee grinder, add the red sugar crystals and grind to a fine powder.

Put the egg whites and cream of tartar in a bowl and whisk until firm peaks form. Whisk in the remaining 100 g scented caster sugar, a spoonful at a time. Gently fold in the pink sugar powder a little at a time.

Spoon 12 piles, about 1 heaped tablespoon each and 5 cm in diameter, onto the baking sheets. Cook in a preheated oven at 110°C (225°F) Gas ¼ for about 1 hour (open the oven door a little if bubbles appear) until firm. Remove from the oven and let cool for 5 minutes, then peel off the paper. Put them back on the paper to cool completely. Store in an airtight container until needed.

To make the chantilly cream, put the cream, icing sugar and rosewater in a bowl and beat until soft peaks form. Use the cream to sandwich the meringues together, then serve sprinkled with crystallized leaves and petals.

thyme (left)

FIG ON A CUSHION WITH THYME-SCENTED SYRUP

500 g puff pastry

6 sprigs of thyme, with flowers if available

75 g caster sugar

2 teaspoons grenadine (pomegranate syrup)

150–200 g triple-crème cheese, such as Saint André, cut horizontally to make 4 discs

6 fresh ripe figs, preferably black (purple), halved vertically

1 egg yolk, beaten with 2 teaspoons water

2 pastry cutters or templates, about 14 cm and 11 cm diameter

serves 4

Pudding and cheese in one, this tart was inspired by chef Paul Gayler from London's Lanesborough Hotel. He uses shortcrust pastry, blue cheese and pears in his version. I use my favourite broad-leaved thyme, the creeping *Thymus pulegioides*. It's in leaf all year round, with beautiful mauve flowers in summer. Orange-scented thyme – *Thymus* 'Fragrantissimus' – would provide another interesting flavour.

Put the pastry on a floured surface and roll out to about 28 cm square. Using the 14 cm pastry cutter or template, cut out 4 circles. Use the edge of the knife to 'knock up' or separate the layers of pastry so they will rise well. Set the circles on the baking sheet and chill for 30 minutes.

Strip the leaves off 4 sprigs of thyme and put them in a small saucepan. Add the sugar and 75 ml water. Set over medium heat and slowly dissolve the sugar. Boil for 4 minutes. Remove from the heat, add the grenadine, let cool, then chill.

Make slashes at 1 cm intervals around the edges of the pastry circles and score an inner circle to join up the slashes, or use the 11 cm pastry cutter – don't cut all the way through. Prick the inside of the inner circle with a fork.

Put 1 round of cheese in the middle of each pastry. Strip the leaves off the remaining 2 sprigs of thyme and sprinkle on top of the cheese. Arrange 3 fig halves on each piece of cheese.

Brush around the edges of the pastry with the beaten egg yolk, but don't let it drip down the sides or the tarts won't rise. Chill until ready to cook. Bake in a preheated oven at 220°C (425°F) Gas 7 for 20–25 minutes until puffed and golden. Strain the scented syrup, pour it over the figs, add a few pink thyme flowers, if using, then serve.

LAVENDER AND TANGERINE ALMOND CAKES

3 mandarins or other small oranges,
such as clementines or tangerines

115 g unsalted butter, cut into small pieces

200 g ground almonds

4 eggs separated

lavender sprigs or petals, to serve

lavender sugar

225 g caster sugar

3 sprigs of lavender stalks

lavender icing

1 teaspoon lavender petals

50 g caster sugar

100 g icing sugar

lavender food colouring (optional)

6 ramekins or dariole moulds, 150 ml each

parchment paper

serves 6

I am a lavender devotee. There was a time when it was seen as the special province of old ladies. Well not any more – it is enjoying a much-deserved renaissance. Its calming and relaxing qualities soothe away pain and encourage tranquil sleep. In the kitchen, its flavour is superb and its colour delightful.

To make the lavender sugar, put the sugar in an airtight container, add the sprigs of lavender and leave overnight. Remove the sprigs before using.

Cut pieces of parchment paper 4 cm higher than the moulds, then use to line them.

Put the whole mandarins in a saucepan, cover with water and simmer for about 30 minutes, taking care not to let them split. Carefully remove and discard the stalks. Drain the mandarins and put them in a blender. Add the butter, almonds and half the lavender sugar and blend until smooth.

Put the remaining lavender sugar in a bowl, add the egg yolks and whisk until pale and thick. Gently fold in the orange mixture.

Put the egg whites in a bowl and beat until soft peaks form. Fold gently into the orange mixture, then use to fill the lined moulds, ½ cm higher than the top of the mould.

Transfer to a preheated oven and bake at 190°C (375°F) Gas 5 for about 40 minutes. To test if they are done, pierce with a skewer – if it comes out clean, they are done. If over-browning, cover and reduce the heat to 180°C (350°F) Gas 4 until done. Remove from the oven, let cool for 10 minutes, then invert onto a wire rack to cool completely.

To make the icing, put the lavender petals and caster sugar in a coffee grinder and work to a fine powder. Sift it and the icing sugar into a bowl, then stir in about 2 tablespoons of water to make a smooth but not too runny icing. If it is too pale, add a tiny drop of food colouring. Turn the cakes the right way up and spoon the icing over the cakes. Top with lavender sprigs or petals and serve. Eat within 2 days.

MOROCCAN MELISSA PASTRIES

200 g shelled pistachios

200 g ground almonds

50 g icing sugar

75 g caster sugar

½ teaspoon ground cinnamon,
plus extra to serve

2 teaspoons rosewater or
orange flower water

a handful of lemon balm (melissa)
or lemon verbena, finely chopped

150 g unsalted butter

8 large sheets of filo pastry

2 tablespoons icing sugar, sifted

a baking sheet

makes 8

This crumbly Moroccan pastry is usually flavoured with mint and finely grated lemon zest. In place of lemon and mint (which you can use instead), I use a close relation of mint – lemon balm – or fragrant lemon verbena, which is in leaf most of the year in my garden. Lemon balm is also known by its pretty name, melissa, from the Greek word for honey bee. It grows like a weed in my garden and I never want to stop it or tame it because it smells so marvellous. It also makes a cool, invigorating drink at the height of summer.

Put the pistachios in a clean coffee grinder and grind to a fine powder. Reserve 2 tablespoons of the pistachio powder to decorate the finished pastries. Put the remainder in a bowl, add the ground almonds, icing sugar, caster sugar, cinnamon, rosewater and lemon balm or lemon verbena.

Soften 100 g of the butter to room temperature and mash into the nut mixture to form a paste. Chill for 10 minutes, then divide into 8 portions.

Melt the remaining butter in a small saucepan. Arrange 1 sheet of filo on a work surface with the long edge towards you (keep the rest covered so it doesn't dry out). Brush the edges of the sheet with melted butter and spread one portion of the paste in a line on the front edge of the filo – leave it loose with a few gaps, so it doesn't split when turned in a spiral. Roll it up, away from you to make a thin log, then brush with a little more butter to make it pliable. Coil the log into a spiral and tuck the end underneath to seal. Brush with extra butter and put on a baking sheet. Repeat to make 8 spirals in total.

Bake in a preheated oven at 200°C (400°F) Gas 6 for 20–25 minutes until golden brown.

Remove from the oven and let cool on a wire rack. Dust with icing sugar, then sprinkle the reserved ground pistachio powder and cinnamon over the top in wriggly lines.

LITTLE EXTRAS

HERB BUTTERS

Herb or 'compound' butters, as they are known, are handy to have in the refrigerator or freezer – just add a spoonful to fish, grilled meat, hot potatoes or other vegetables. The flavours trapped in the butter are a revelation, so experiment with different herbs. Here are some ideas to start you off!

CHIVRY BUTTER

a large bunch of mixed herbs such as parsley, tarragon, chervil, salad burnet and chives, about 65 g

150 g salted butter

1½ tablespoons finely chopped shallot

makes 250 ml

Strip the leaves off the stalks and blanch in a saucepan of boiling water for 30 seconds. Tip into a colander and refresh under cold running water.

Drain, pat dry and chop coarsely. Melt 2 tablespoons of the butter in a small frying pan, add the shallot and cook over low heat until slightly softened but not browned, about 2 minutes. Let cool.

Pour into a food processor, then add the herbs and remaining butter. Pulse until smooth, then transfer to a sheet of greaseproof paper or clingfilm and roll into a log. Alternatively, spoon into little butter dishes, smooth off the tops with a knife, then chill until firm.

NASTURTIUM AND SAVORY BUTTER

5 sprigs of savory

8 nasturtium leaves

8 nasturtium flowers

150 g salted butter

makes 200 ml

Strip the leaves from the savory and chop them finely. Chop the nasturtium leaves and flowers. Put in a food processor with the butter and pulse to mix.

BASIL, PINE NUT AND CHILLI BUTTER

50 g pine nuts, lightly toasted in a dry frying pan

4 tablespoons chopped basil leaves

1 small red chilli, deseeded and finely chopped

150 g salted butter

makes 300 ml

Put the pine nuts in a small food processor, then grind as finely as possible. Add the remaining ingredients and pulse to mix. Transfer to a sheet of greaseproof paper or clingfilm and roll into a log. Alternatively, spoon into little butter dishes, smooth off the tops with a knife, then chill until firm.

EXTRA IDEAS

- Dill leaves and salted anchovy fillets
- Mint and fresh pomegranate juice
- Lovage and walnuts
- Fennel leaves and rose petals

- coriander
- curry leaves or bay leaves (optional)
- mint

MINT AND CORIANDER SALSA
WITH SINGARAS

500 g potatoes suitable for mashing, cut into chips

8 curry leaves or 3 bay leaves

1 tablespoon vegetable oil, plus extra for deep-frying

2 onions, finely chopped

2 garlic cloves, crushed

2 hottish green chillies, deseeded and finely chopped

1 teaspoon ground cumin

a small bunch of coriander leaves, chopped

16 small spring roll wrappers (13 cm square), cut in 2 or 8 large (25 cm square), cut in 3

sea salt

salsa

5 pink Thai shallots or 2 regular shallots, finely chopped

finely grated zest and juice of 1 unwaxed lime

½ teaspoon sugar (optional)

2 ripe mangoes, peeled and cut into small cubes

2 red chillies, deseeded and finely chopped

a small bunch of mint, finely chopped

a small bunch of coriander, finely chopped

an electric deep-fryer (optional)

serves 6–8

Singaras are a kind of Indian samosa, but I make them with spring roll wrappers rather than heavier pastry. They are wonderful on their own, with a squeeze of lemon, or with a salsa like this one. Another idea is to put whole coriander and mint leaves, and finely sliced red onion into small bowls, so people can take a little of each with a bite of singara – the result is a terrific snack to serve with drinks. Make them large or small.

Put the freshly cut potato chips in a saucepan of cold water, add the curry leaves or bay leaves, bring to the boil, then add salt. When the potatoes are soft, drain and cover with a clean tea towel for 5 minutes, then remove the curry leaves and chop into the potatoes. If using bay leaves, discard them. Put the potatoes in a bowl.

Heat the oil in a frying pan, add the onions and garlic and fry until soft and very pale golden. Mash the potatoes, then stir in the onions, garlic, chillies, cumin and chopped coriander. Stir briefly and let cool.

Put a strip of spring roll wrapper on a work surface and put a teaspoon of mixture in the bottom left hand corner. Fold over to the right to make a triangle. Continue folding, end to end, then wet the edge with a little water and press to seal.

Fill a wok or deep-fryer one-third full with oil, or to the manufacturer's recommended level, and heat to 200°C (400°F). Add the singaras in batches of 2–3 and fry for about 2 minutes each, turning occasionally. Remove and drain on kitchen paper while you cook the remainder. They can be made in advance, and reheated in the oven, or served cold.

To make the salsa, put the shallots in a bowl, add the lime zest and juice, and sugar, if using, and set aside for 5 minutes. Just before serving, stir in the mangoes, chillies, mint and coriander. Serve with the singaras.

- basil
- thyme

TOMSATINA CHUTNEY
WITH BASIL AND THYME

24 ripe, well-flavoured vine tomatoes, about 2.25 kg

10 banana shallots, finely chopped, about 300 g

3 tablespoons yellow mustard seeds

1 tablespoon allspice berries

2 tablespoons thyme leaves

250 g caster sugar

300 ml cider vinegar

a large bunch of basil, chopped

sea salt and freshly ground black pepper

4 preserving jars, 450 g each

makes 1.8 kg

This is one of my mother's favourite pickles, especially when there are lots of tomatoes and basil around. The chutney is good to eat with strong organic farmhouse Cheddar-style cheese. In summer, just as the thyme is flowering, you should prune it hard, so it has another growth spurt before autumn. Then use the cuttings for recipes like these. Basil should be in full flavour at the same time.

Cut the tomatoes in half, cut out the cores and chop the flesh. Put in a jam pan and add the shallots and mustard seeds. Wrap the allspice in muslin and add to the pan. Cook over gentle heat until the tomato juices start to run. Add the thyme, increase the heat and simmer for about 45 minutes, until reduced by about one-third.

Add the sugar and lower the heat until it dissolves. Add salt, pepper, vinegar and basil. Increase the heat again and simmer until it thickens, about 30 minutes. Remove the muslin-wrapped allspice berries.

To bottle the chutney you will need some sterilized jars. To sterilize jars, line the jars up in a sink and pour boiling water into them. Let to stand for 5 minutes, then carefully pour the water out. Put the jars in a low oven to dry. Transfer the hot jars onto a board lined with paper (easy to throw away if you spill anything). Use a bottling funnel to fill the jars while the chutney is still hot, but not boiling. Cover immediately with a circle of waxed paper and the lid. Tighten the lid when the chutney has cooled down a little.

Cook's extra This chutney is also good with 1 tablespoon of chopped black olives folded into about 5 tablespoons of chutney before serving. Serve with a young pecorino cheese and crisp Italian *carta de musica* as a snack with drinks.

HERB VINEGARS

There are two methods for making herb infused vinegars. Either push a sprig or two into the bottle and replace the lid, or boil 500 ml vinegar for every 65 g of herb leaves. Pour over the leaves, set aside to infuse for 2 weeks, then strain and pour into sterilized bottles (page 137) and seal with tight-fitting corks.

• Flavour white wine vinegar with tarragon

• Red wine vinegar with rosemary

• Cider vinegar with apple mint

• Rice vinegar with Thai sweet basil

• Champagne vinegar with rose petals or rose geranium leaves

• Push lavender flowers on long stems into bottles of white wine vinegar and leave on a window sill in full sun – the result is a delicious vinegar for salad dressing

HERB OILS

Any herb can be used to flavour oil, especially if you have large quantities of a particular herb in the garden and the hot sun has strengthened the volatile oils. I prefer to use the best quality extra virgin olive oil, but any olive oil would do.

• The method for most woody herbs and tender leaves is simply to put a sprig or two in the bottle and leave until the flavour is to your liking.

• For soft herbs like basil, pull the leaves from a large bunch, plunge them into boiling water, drain and instantly refresh under cold running water. Dry thoroughly on kitchen paper. Put the leaves and 300 ml olive oil in a blender and blend well. Transfer the resulting purée to a bowl and leave to infuse overnight. Strain the wonderful bright green oil through a muslin-lined sieve, pour into sterilized bottles (page 137) and store in the refrigerator. It can be used straight away or within 10 days.

TISANES

A tisane is a herb tea, made with herbs, spices or flowers infused in boiling water. For centuries, they have been used to treat illnesses, soothe the nerves, wake people up, or just because they taste good. Try these time-honoured favourites.

• Tulsi tisane is made of bush basil or holy basil, called *tulsi* in India. It is a holy plant and was Krishna's favourite. He preferred the humble tulsi leaf to any of the flowers in the garden. In India, it isn't used for any purposes other than those of a spiritual nature – so I include this recipe for holy herbal tea given to me by a friend from an ashram near the ancient Indian city of Rishikesh.

Put a handful of basil leaves and the zest of 1 unwaxed orange in a teapot, add 600 ml boiling water and leave to infuse. Serve sweetened with 2 teaspoons honey (optional).

• Hyssop tisane is said to be good for colds in the chest.

Put a handful of hyssop leaves in a teapot, add 600 ml boiling water and leave to infuse. Serve sweetened with 2 teaspoons of honey (optional).

Variations

• Ginger tea or **peppermint** tea will soothe an upset stomach

• **Lemon balm** (melissa) tea will invigorate

• **Rosemary**, especially when infused with honey, not only tastes good but helps with physical and mental strain (and is better for you than that caffeine-laden cappuccino)

• Another morning reviver is **lemon verbena** with **peppermint** and rose petals

OTHER THINGS TO DO WITH HERBS ...

• Don't forget the flowers from your herbs such as **basil** or **marjoram**. Sprinkle them over dishes before serving – they are all edible, full of flavour and very pretty.

• Keep stalks of **parsley** and **chervil** to add to stocks, when boiling potatoes and vegetables, or to infuse in cream for sauces.

• Stalks and roots of **coriander** hold a lot of flavour, so in many dishes I chop most of the stalk and include it, too. When you buy coriander in Asian and Middle Eastern markets, the roots will still be intact. Use them to make Thai curry paste, but freeze them if you can't use them straight away.

• Use **rosemary** and **bay leaf** stalks as kebab skewers.

• Branches of **fennel, rosemary, bay leaves, thyme, oregano** and **marjoram** are all delicious when thrown on the dying embers of a barbecue. Remember, you want smoke not flame to flavour the food, so add them just before the food is completely cooked otherwise the flames will blacken it. Alternatively, push them into the cavity of a fish or chicken to flavour the flesh before cooking.

• Make ice cubes with whole herb leaves and chive flowers (left) to drop into water jugs. **Borage** flowers are beautiful used this way.

• Chop leaves and flowers and freeze in ice cube trays for stocks and soups.

• Crystallize leaves such as **scented geraniums, mint, sweet cicely, basil, lemon balm** and **pineapple sage**, and the petals and flowers of roses, **borage**, violas and violets. Paint them with lightly whisked egg white and dust with caster sugar, place on a wire rack lined with parchment paper and put in a warm dry place to harden. Store in an airtight container until ready to use.

• Strew handfuls of **chervil**, young **parsley, basil, mint** and **coriander** leaves on top of dishes, then fold in just before serving.

• Wilt soft, young leaves of **oregano, chervil, parsley, tarragon, shiso** or **basil** into hot pasta.

• Roast peanuts or cashews and, while still burning hot, sprinkle with chillies and lots of **Chinese chives** and their flowers for a pre-barbecue snack with cold beer.

• Make thin sandwiches with fresh wholemeal bread, thick butter and handfuls of soft herbs, such as **parsley, chervil, basil, tarragon** and **watercress**. Cut into squares to eat with herbal tea or just as a little snack with some real lemonade on a picnic.

• Use **thyme, fennel** or **rosemary** to flavour jars of olives in oil.

• Serve mixed bowls of **tarragon, mint, basil, parsley** and **watercress** – in fact, any soft-leaf mixture – with wedges of feta and flat crispbread. An old Iranian tradition tells women to eat this at the end of a meal to keep their men from the attentions of rivals.

• Make fresh Herbes de Provence with **thyme, savory, oregano** and **hyssop**.

• Chop **lavender** flowers and roast with root vegetables.

Bouquets garnis are traditional flavourings for casseroles:

• To make a bouquet garni for meat, make a bunch of 2 sprigs of **parsley**, 4 sprigs of **thyme**, 2 **bay leaves** and 1 celery stalk, then tie together with string. Discard before serving.

• To make a bouquet garni for fish, make a bunch of 4 sprigs of **fennel**, 4 sprigs of **parsley** and 4 sprigs of **marjoram**, then tie together with string. Discard before serving.

• To make a bouquet garni for chicken, make a bunch of 4 sprigs of **tarragon**, 2 **bay leaves**, a strip of fennel or celery, then tie together with string. Discard before serving.

Herb-flavoured vodka is a 500-year-old tradition:

• Put 6 sprigs of **tarragon** into a bottle of vodka. Infuse for 36 hours at room temperature. Strain out and discard the leaves, then freeze the vodka for at least 5 hours before drinking.

• Put a handful of **wild garlic** with flowers into a bottle of vodka and proceed as above. Add a few fresh star-like wild garlic flowers to the bottle before freezing for a touch of glamour.

MAIL ORDER AND WEBSITES

HERBS, PLANTS AND SEEDS

Arne Herbs
Limeburn Nurseries,
Limeburn Hill, Chew Magna,
Bristol BS40 8QW
Tel. 01275 333399
www.arneherbs.co.uk
*Suppliers of traditional, medicinal,
Renaissance, medieval, Tudor and rare
herbs worldwide. Wild flower
conservation. Rare and culinary herbs.*

Chesters' Walled Garden
Tel. 01434 681483
www.chesterswalledgarden.co.uk
*No catalogue: no mail order, but seeds
sold from their shop. Situated next to
Chesters Roman Fort, on the line of
Hadrian's Wall. National collection of
thymes and marjorams and includes a
Roman garden. Opening times: 10 am –
5 pm daily, 1 April to 31 October.
Opening times from November to end of
March depend on the weather (phone first).*

City Herbs
1 Spital House
New Spitalfields Market
Leyton Accounts, London E10 5SQ
Tel. 020 8558 9708
www.cityherbs.co.uk
*Supplies top London restaurants, has a
refrigerated warehouse in Britain's busiest
wholesale market, scores of products
grown exclusively for it.*

Cool Chile Company
West Dean Gardens, West Sussex
Tel. 01243 818209 for details
Tel. 0870 902 1145
www.coolchile.co.uk
Epazote seed and Mexican goods.

English Cottage Garden Nursery
Herons, Giggers Green Road
Aldington TN25 7BU
Tel. 01233 720907
Fax. 01233 720907
http://www.englishplants.co.uk
*A small nursery growing traditional
cottage garden plants, wildflowers and
herbs. Situated in Kent, on the edge of
Romney Marsh, beside the Royal Military
Canal. Visiting by appointment only. All
plants grown in peat-free, coir compost.*

Foxhollow Nurseries
73 Lower Pillory Downs,
Little Woodcoat Estate,
Carshalton, Surrey FM5 4DD
Tel. 020 8660 0991

Halcyon Seeds
10 Hampden Close,
Chalgrove, Oxford OX44 7SB
Tel/Fax. 01865 890180
www.halcyonseeds.co.uk
*A partnership between experienced
grower Richard Bartlett and ex-chef Bob
Griffin. Richard, who specializies in
unusual salad leaves, was the original
head gardener for Raymond Blanc at Le
Manoir Aux Quat' Saisons near Oxford.
Offers a selection of salad leaf, vegetable
and herb seed that will yield good results
for the kitchen gardener. All the seed is
untreated or organic.*

Iden Croft Herbs
International Herb Centre of Kent
Frittenden Road, Staplehurst, Kent TN12
Tel. 01580 891 432
Fax. 01580 892 416
www.herbs-uk.com
*Established over 30 years in the grounds
of a former Augustinian Friary. The walled
garden is Tudor. Later, the land formed
part of the Staplehurst Manor estate. The
kitchen gardens, orchard, hot houses etc.
were on the area which now form Iden
Croft Herbs.*

Jekka's Herb Farm
Rose Cottage, Shellards Lane,
Alveston, Bristol BS35 3SY
Tel. 01454 418878
Fax. 01454 411988
www.jekkasherbfarm.com
*Catalogue is available on request. The
farm holds 8 open days per year, but is
not open to the public on a daily basis.*

Laurel Farm Herbs
Main Road, Kelsale Road,
Suffolk IP17 2RG
Tel. 01728 668223
www.laurelfarmherbs.co.uk
Growing herbs delivered to your door.

Marshalls Vegetable Seed Company
S.E. Marshalls & Co. Ltd,
Freepost PE787, Wisbech,
Cambs PE13 2WE
Tel. 01945 466711
www.marshalls-seeds.co.uk
All you need for the kitchen garden.

The Organic Gardening Catalogue
Riverdene, Molesey Road,
Hersham
Surrey KT12 4RG
Tel. 01932 253666
www.OrganicCatalog.com
Organic seeds including herbs, salads.

Simpson's Seeds
The Walled Garden Nursery,
Frome Road, Horningsham,
Somerset BA12 7NQ
Tel. 01985 845004
Salad vegetables including chillies.

Suffolk Herbs (plants and seeds)
Monks Farm, Kelvedon
Colchester
Essex CO5 9PG
Tel. 01376 572456
www.suffolkherbs.com
Salad vegetables and organic seeds.

ASIAN FOODS AND HERBS

Asian Food Suppliers
Sri Thai (Thai)
56 Shepherd's Bush Road,
London W6 7PH
Tel. 020 7602 0621

Super Bahar (Iranian and Middle Eastern)
349 Kensington High Street,
London W8 6NW
Tel. 020 7603 5083

Talad Thai (Thai, South-east Asian)
320 Upper Richmond Road,
London SW15 6TL
Tel. 020 8789 8084

Paya Thai (Thai)
101–103 Kew Road,
Richmond TW9 2PN
www.payathai.co.uk

Tawana Oriental Supermarket (Thai)
18 Chepstow Road,
London W2 5BD
Tel. 020 7221 6316

Atari-Ya
7 Station Parade, Noel Road
London W3 ODS
Tel. 020 8896 1552
*Japanese shiso leaves and sahimi-quality
seafood*

Thanh Xuân Supermarket (Vietnamese)
84 Deptford High Street
London SE8 4RG
Tel. 020 8691 8106

TK Trading (Japanese)
Unit 7, The Chase Centre, Chase Road,
North Acton
London NW10 6QD
Tel. 020 8453 1743/1001
www.japan-foods.co.uk (in Japanese)
Email: tktrade@uk2.so-net.com

ASIAN SPECIALIST FOOD DISTRICTS

Southall, Tooting and Wembley
*Three areas full of Indian, Bangladeshi
and Pakistani grocers and shops,
stocking a wide range of South Asian
spices and ingredients.*

Edgware Road, London
*Lebanese and Middle Eastern spices and
ingredients.*

Gerrard Street area, Soho, London
Chinese and Asian ingredients.

NATURAL PEST CONTROL

The Green Gardener
1 Whitmore Wood, Rendlesham
Suffolk IP12 2US
Tel/Fax. 01394 420087
www.greengardener.co.uk
*Mail order source for ladybirds, lacewings
and natural forms of pest control.
Includes wormeries, worms for the
garden, home composting, wildlife homes
and feeders, biological control of slugs,
vine weevil, aphids – leatherjackets,
chafer grubs, whitefly, encarsia and
much more.*

INDEX

CL265519